T0309870

Machinic Eros

Félix Guattari
edited by Gary Genosko and Jay Hetrick

Machinic Eros: Writings on Japan
by Félix Guattari

Edited by Gary Genosko and Jay Hetrick

First Edition
Minneapolis © 2015, Univocal Publishing

"Pathic Transferences and Contemporary Japanese Art" © Gary Genosko
"Toward a Critical Nomadism? Félix Guattari in Japan" © Jay Hetrick

Published by Univocal
123 North 3rd Street, #202
Minneapolis, MN 55401

Thanks to Les Enfants Guattari, Keiichi Tahara, Imec,
Tetsuo Kogawa, Toshiya Ueno, Iloe Ariss

Designed & Printed by Jason Wagner

Distributed by the University of Minnesota Press

ISBN 9781937561208
Library of Congress Control Number 2014954837

Table of Contents

Part I
Writings on Japan by Félix Guattari

Tokyo, the Proud..13

Translocal: Tetsuo Kogawa Interviews Félix Guattari................17

Butoh..43

Body-Assemblage: Félix Guattari and Min Tanaka in Dialogue......45

Keiichi Tahara's Faciality Machines....................................55

The "always never seen" of Keiichi Tahara...........................67

Imai: Painter of Chaosmosis...71

The Rich Affects of Madam Yayoi Kusama...................................75

The Architectural Machines of Shin Takamatsu..........................77

Singularization and Style:
Shin Takamatsu in Conversation with Félix Guattari................87

Ecosophical Practices
and the Restoration of the "Subjective City"................................97

Part II
Critical Essays

Pathic Transferences and Contemporary Japanese Art
By Gary Genosko..119

Toward a Critical Nomadism? Félix Guattari in Japan
By Jay Hetrick..137

Original Publication Data

For permission to reprint and/or translate material, the editors and publisher are grateful to the following:

Tokyo, the Proud
trans. Gary Genosko and Tim Adams
© Bruno, Emmanuelle, Stephen Guattari - Fonds Imec
Originally published in *Deleuze Studies* 1.2 (December 2007), pp. 96-99.

Translocal: Tetsuo Kogawa Interviews Félix Guattari
trans. Adam Colin Chambers, revised by Jay Hetrick
© Tetsuo Kogawa / © Bruno, Emmanuelle, and Stephen Guattari - Fonds Imec
Partially published in *Hype_Text* #1(Autumn 2000), pp. 1-12. Interviews conducted on 18 and 24 October 1980 and 22 May 1981 (Tokyo, Japan).

Butoh
trans. Gary Genosko
© Bruno, Emmanuelle, and Stephen Guattari - Fonds Imec
Originally published in Félix Guattari, *Les Années d'Hiver: 1980-1985* (Paris: Les prairies ordinaires, 2009), p. 266. Presentation of a Butoh dance program by Min Tanaka, 1984.

Body-Assemblage: Félix Guattari and Min Tanaka in Dialogue
trans. Toshiya Ueno and Toulouse-Antonin Roy
© Min Tanaka / © Bruno, Emmanuelle, and Stephen Guattari - Fonds Imec
Originally published in Min Tanaka and Félix Guattari, *Velocity of Light, Fire of Zen: Assemblage 85*, Shuukanbon Weekly Book 35 (June 1985), pp. 9-33.

Keiichi Tahara's Faciality Machines
trans. Andrew Goffey
© Bruno, Emmanuelle et Stephen Guattari - Fonds Imec
Originally published in Félix Guattari, *Schizoanalytic Cartographies*, trans. Andrew Goffey (London: Bloomsbury, 2013), pp. 247-252.

The "always never seen" of Keiichi Tahara
trans. Jay Hetrick
© Bruno, Emmanuelle, and Stephen Guattari - Fonds Imec
Originally published in Félix Guattari, *Les Années d'Hiver: 1980-1985* (Paris: Les prairies ordinaires, 2009), pp. 267-69. Bulletin of the French Book published by the Embassy of France in Tokyo, 1st quarter 1985.

Imai: Painter of Chaosmosis
trans. Jay Hetrick
© Bruno, Emmanuelle, and Stephen Guattari - Fonds Imec
Originally published in Toshimitsu Imai, *Imai: Hiroshima* (Tokyo: Gallery Gan, 1997), pp. 16-17.

The Rich Affects of Madam Yayoi Kusama
trans. Gary Genosko
© Bruno, Emmanuelle, and Stephen Guattari - Fonds Imec
IMEC ET 06-19 Fonds Guattari. Typescript, 2 pages, no date.

The Architectural Machines of Shin Takamatsu
trans. Tim Adams and Catherine Howell, revised by Jay Hetrick
© Bruno, Emmanuelle, and Stephen Guattari - Fonds Imec
Originally published in *Chimères* 21 (Winter 1994), pp. 127-41.

Singularization and Style: Shin Takamatsu in Conversation with Félix Guattari
trans. Wayne Lawrence and Elizabeth Cheng
© Bruno, Emmanuelle, and Stephen Guattari -Fonds Imec
Originally published in *Parallax* 7.4 (2001), pp. 131-137.

Ecosophical Practices and the Restoration of the "Subjective City"
trans. Kuniichi Uno *et al.*, revised by Gary Genosko
© Japan Institute of Architects / Bruno, Emmanuelle, Stephen Guattari - Fonds Imec
Originally published as "Restoration of the Urban Landscape" in Riichi Miyake, ed., *Proposal from Nagoya* (Nagoya: Japan Institute of Architects, 1989), pp. 85-95. The conference talk was augmented for publication by Guattari. This translation by Gary Genosko follows, with some of Guattari's interpolations from his talk in Nagoya remaining, the longer version published in *Chimères* 17 (1992), pp. 1-18.

Part I
Machinic Eros:
Writings on Japan by Félix Guattari

Machinic Eros

Tokyo, the Proud

Luminous cubes[1] on top of the skyscrapers. To blaze a trail across the sky? To interpellate the gods? Certainly, out of pride, like the medieval towers of Bologna.

That inimitable attentiveness of your Japanese interlocutor who suddenly makes you feel worthy of consideration and induces you into the mimetic temptation – irresistible, though hopeless – of understanding the other from a viewpoint imbued with a new sensitivity.

An imperceptible transgression is then followed by rejection and abandonment on the shores of a final void. Pride, gentleness and violence mingle in the fleeting exchange of glances [*fleur de regard*].

Paradoxically, female and maternal values are omnipresent yet so rigorously circumscribed and inhibited; this makes their repression ostentatious.

---

1. The obvious, but misleading, reference is to Shin Takamatsu's Kirin Plaza (1987) in Osaka. The luminous cubes are the four patterned rectangular lanterns that reach toward the sky from the four corners of the structure. This building is not in Tokyo; so, any of the dazzling neon towers of Shinjuku or Shibuya will suffice. One is struck by the image of Guattari wandering around the nocturnal city fixated on the bright spectacle above his head. The same sense is found in his *Ritournelles*, this time with respect to the dense, hypermodern commercial district in Tokyo, Shinjuku: "The buildings of Shinjuku traversed from top to bottom by parallel neon bars." *La Nouvelle Revue Française* 549 (April 1999), p. 337. [TN]

Three-tiered concrete highways span the mosaic city, legs wide apart like the heroes of the Kabuki theater, crushing all in their path. Each day thousands of additional inhabitants and hundreds of conquering companies are parachuted in; the absurd lamination of the urban patrimony.

I don't know how many "mountaineers" risk their lives climbing the most inaccessible peaks of the Himalayas each year, I only recall that more than half of them are Japanese.

What is it that drives the Japanese? Is it the attraction of wealth and luxury, the consequences of the marked lack of iron affecting their memories?[2] Or, perhaps it is primarily the desire to be "in the thick of things" [*être dans le coup*], what I call machinic eros!

Becoming a child of Japan; becoming Japanese of our future childhoods.

Certainly do not confuse these becomings with capitalistic infantilism and its vibrating zones of collective hysteria, such as the syndrome of puerile cute culture (*kawaii*), the reading-drug of Manga comics, or the intrusiveness of loukoum music; the latter is, to my taste, the worst kind of pollution.[3]

All the trends of the West have arrived on the shores of these islands without resistance. But the wave of Judeo-Christian guilt that feeds our "spirit of capitalism" has never managed to swamp them. Might Japanese capitalism be a mutation resulting from the monstrous crossing of animist powers inherited from feudalism during the "Baku-han" and the machinic powers of modernity to which it appears everything here must revert?

Externalized interiorities and rebellious exteriorities with univocal signifying reductions populate the surfaces and engender new depths of the sort where inside and outside no longer maintain the mutually exclusive relationship of opposition to which Westerners are accustomed. The signalizing [*signalétiques*] matters characteristic of the texture of subjectivity are found to be

---

2. Guattari exploits here the medical link between iron deficiency and impaired memory [*manque marquée du fer dans les mémoires* – marked lack of iron affecting their memories] in a double entendre. [TN]

3. Guattari appears to be complaining about a kind of electronic music, a species of techno known as *loukoum* in France and elsewhere. It is named after the sweet "Turkish Delight." [TN]

inextricably related to the energetico-spatio-temporal components of the urban fabric.

Despite the cancerous tumors that threaten to suffocate it at any moment, Tokyo in many ways reveals its ancient existential territories and ancestral affinities between microcosm and macrocosm. This is apparent at the level of its primary configurations, whose admirable oneiric explorations have been presented to us by Kobo Abe's novel *The Ruined Map*,[4] as well as in the molecular behavior of its crowds that appear to treat public spaces as so many private domains.

Is it enough to say that the ancient surfaces of Yin and Yang, raw and cooked, analogical iconicity and "digital" discursivity, still manage to merge opposites? Or, further, that today the Japanese brain reconciles its right and left hemispheres according to specific modalities, or any other such unsound and harmful nonsense in which a number of anthropologists seem to delight?

Different approaches that are less archaizing and less simplistic could perhaps lead us to a better understanding of the present form of this Japanese pride. A Manichean affirmation rises to the surface everywhere in the reigning phallocratism, in a will to thoroughly exploit, sometimes to the point of absurdity, the tyrannical power of shame associated with any infringement of the exterior signs of the dominant conformity.

And what about this cult of the norm, this "canonism" that is cultivated like a fine art, and harbors a fundamental heterodoxy of secret dissidences? Is it merely the facade and medium in aid of imperceptible singularizations – at the very least from Western viewpoints?

The deterritorialized mandalas in intimate gestures of similitude; the unmentionable pleasures in the respect for etiquette, punctuality, and submission to rituals which dissipate vague yearnings, and circumscribe the wandering of fuzzy intentionalities…. From small differences proliferate – far removed from egoic harmonies – large-scale collective undertakings [*projectualités*].

---

4. Kobo Abe, *The Ruined Map*, trans. E. Dale Saunders (New York: Vintage, 1997). Guattari was an avid reader of Abe novels and found the dream cartography of the aforementioned detective novel particularly evocative of a marginal Tokyo. [TN]

But these just as easily trap the molecular capitalistic machineries which, in order to temporarily divert Japanese elites from the territorialized hedonism of the historical bourgeoisie, threaten to sink them yet again, in a deathly will to power.

At the invitation of the "Aid and Mutual Action Committee" of Sanya,[5] I traveled to the place where the Yakuzas assassinated Mitsuo Sato,[6] and paid homage to this progressive filmmaker who investigated the Japan of the disenfranchised, precarious and rebellious.

Kobo Abe remarked on the fact that Sanya is perhaps less representative of an absolute misery than an irrevocable refusal of the existing order. He declared that he would like to "be worthy of Sanya."

Vertigo of another Japanese way: Tokyo relinquishes its status as the Eastern capital of Western capitalism in order to become the Northern capital of the emancipation of the Third World.

---

5. Sanya is a district in Tokyo in which foreign and day laborers live. Many are homeless and live in makeshift shelters made of found materials. Elsewhere Guattari simply made the point that zones of disparity coexist in the great cities, no more in terms of center and periphery relations, citing the concentrated wealth of Shinjuku and misery of Sanya as an example. See "Space and Corporeity: Drawing/Cities/Nomads" in *Semiotext(e) Architecture* (1992), pp. 118–21, 122–25. [TN]

6. Mitsuo Sato was a Japanese documentary film director known for his social activism. He was murdered during the making of his 1985 film "YAMA," the colloquial name for Sanya. The film follows the struggles of the district's day laborers to organize. [TN]

Translocal: Tetsuo Kogawa interviews Félix Guattari

Part I: October 18, 1980

Tetsuo Kogawa: Let me introduce myself. As early as 1973, one year after *Anti-Oedipus* was published – which created a stir in our study group on contemporary radical ideas – I became familiar with your work, but I didn't think a great deal about it until 1975 when I visited New York. Since then, I have become a regular "commuter" to New York. There, I not only became more familiar with your articles through various journals such as *Substance*, *Diacritics*, and *Semiotext(e)*, but I also realized that "organic negativity" – i.e., traditional oppositional forces – have been increasingly declining and exhausted in proportion to the great growth of federal bureaucracy, the ever stronger rise of multinationals, and the deeper permeation of advanced communication and advertising techniques into everyday life. In this situation, it has become more and more difficult to rely on previous revolutionary forms of collectivity and, worse still, even anti-establishment groups can be utilized by the dominant system as a kind of internal regulatory mechanism. Furthermore, the system (there might be slight differences between popular and communist states) does not hesitate to invent such a mechanism within the system, artificial negativity in Paul Piccone's terms. A similar trend, on a smaller scale but in a more concentrated facade, is appearing. I want to apply this point to recent Japan as well. However, it is in this very situation that I have found the real relevance of your analysis and strategy of micropolitics and permanent attempts in organizations being conscious of your basic notions of multiplicity, desiring production, transversality, and so on. The fact is that the more subtle the dominant system of control becomes, the more relevant your analyses and critiques are. This is how I became familiar with your ideas and theories. Well, I would like to ask you my first question: what is the relationship between your concepts of micropolitics and macropolitics?

Félix Guattari: I believe it is first necessary to distinguish between levels of the microsocial and the macrosocial. So, the size of the social groups under consideration. And also between questions of the micropolitical and the macropolitical or, in other terms, the politics of the *molecular* and the *molar*.

Kogawa: Ok, I wonder how micropolitics relates to macropolitics?

Guattari: A macropolitical phenomenon of great scale, for example the programs of Mr. Carter, or Giscard D'Estaing, or Tanaka – the electoral program in short – can have absolutely no practical efficiency. Whereas, on the other hand, mircopolitical struggles – for example the feminist movement, the homosexual movement, and the movement of alternative psychiatry – which all appear to have little effect at the macropolitical level – can in fact produce effects of great magnitude on the scale of an entire country or even the whole planet. It's for this reason that I say we must firmly underline the fact that a micropolitical transformation, in what I call the *molecular unconscious*, can change a situation understood at the historical level or at the level Fernand Braudel calls "the long-term," whereas great social and political struggles at the molar scale can only produce local effects and events but cannot truly change the social fabric.

Kogawa: One thing I don't understand is the recent reactionary trend in Europe, especially in Italy, where the seemingly old-fashioned repression and absurd exercises of the police have become rampant. I wonder whether this trend is a mere retrogression of the power system, which fails to control civil society in a soft and subtle way, or a new advanced type of domination. Also, is it possible to suppose that today's repressive European trend derives from a lack of self-regulating flexibility such as the American system has?

Guattari: First of all, I am not convinced that the difference you've highlighted between Europe and the United States will continue for much longer. I think we have to accept the idea that there will be a coexistence between two systems: a system of soft, fluid social control and a system of increasingly harsh repression, which liquidates all the old democratic systems, the systems of judicial independence and a certain number of procedures guaranteeing individual rights. I think this is a general phenomenon in the evolution of Integrated World Capitalism. The work of the Trilateral Commission has also explicitly stated that there's an incompatibility between a certain level of democratic freedom and a restructuring at the level of contemporary capitalism. I would like to add two points here. First of all, it seems that all the neo-liberal illusions of the American economists will fall and collapse into ruin. The modern evolution of capitalism will not necessarily drive toward progress in the sense of democracy and social improvement. Secondly, I think we have to revise the old conceptions of the struggle for freedoms that still persist today. These are conceptions that revive bourgeois democracy. They are not fundamental objectives for the struggles of the working class or for the struggles of revolutionaries. I think that the struggles for the defense of laws, for an independent judiciary, and against a repression that is, in many respects, illegal in Italy, in France, etc., have become absolute and fundamental points. And one more thing in conclusion. The struggle for the rights of man is important for the countries of the Soviet Union, China, etc., but it is also extremely important within capitalist countries themselves.

Kogawa: In terms of such apparatuses, I completely agree with you. But I wonder why governments have to use such harsh techniques of repression such as police force and so on?

Guattari: In my opinion, the fundamental question and what is brought to light by current capitalist tendencies is a certain truth about capitalism, which perhaps we didn't see very clearly before. Capitalism is not only a process to extract economic value, of added value, through the process of wage-labor. Capitalism is essentially a system that wants to extract power in order to consolidate a certain type of social segregation and social segmentation. The economic means of wage-earners is just one element among the different means of capitalistic intervention. There are indeed other elements that put into play the freedom of movement: the segregation between genders, between races, between ages, between those who possess knowledge and culture and those who do not have access, etc. Today capitalism is very interested in the production of automobiles as well as surplus values it can extract from large branches of industry, but it's also interested in the production of mass media, the production of the libido, and the establishment of a general social grid. All these form a part of its overall project. Previously, it was thought that capitalism was simply interested in heavy industry, in Renault factories. Well today it is – equally and fundamentally – interested in everything that concerns culture and mass media. And today the situation worsens, the contradictions worsen, and the problem is not to further extract and exploit the workforce – from this point of view it has resolved its problems – but rather to guarantee a type of control that is increasingly pronounced in its formations of power. These are the problems, the contradictions today. It is not so much a question of wages, a question of the labor-time of workers, a question of extraction of the work force, of exploitation in the sense of the Marxist formula of extracting the most surplus value. One could imagine that they double the salaries or that they cut the working day in half for workers in Japan, in Germany, in the United States. Capitalism will not perish over this. The real problems are the billions of people on this earth who are dying of famine, a certain type of oppression against women, the lack of hope or perspective for the young, and the absurdity of the system. These are the true problems of capitalism and it's there, above us, where it won't let go. The real question then concerns the limits of desire and therefore, by extension, the question of a *molecular revolution*.

Kogawa: Very interesting. Can we suppose that the foundation of this social grid is the family?

Guattari: Not only.

Kogawa: But isn't the most virulent foundation of gridding the family? In the US, as far as I know, a kind of disorganizing phenomenon through the family has been rapidly developing. Nobody can control it. But there is also a new form of control: that of media, video, and television. This new type of control makes the best use of strategic market techniques. And, in order to liberate our repressed desires, to overcome familism itself, radicals in the US are very much interested in the homosexual movement, which intentionally disorganizes family structure.

Guattari: Obviously all of these areas are brought into question – the couple, the family, domestic life, are all very important – but I think we need to be careful not to fall into a trap here. There are many other areas to be taken into consideration as well. On the one hand, we have what I call "infrapersonal components": those that concern the body, the super-ego, law, repression, the creation of the self. And on the other hand, we have all the other domains of life – social and "suprapersonal" – that concern education, culture, music, sports, etc. It's a comprehensive phenomenon and the Americans have a bit of a tendency to seek, with their pragmatism, a miracle solution. For some, it's transcendental meditation. For others, it's the improvement of intra-familial communication. It's one technique or another. In fact, it concerns not only a problem of local technique, but also a problem of the general transformation of existing molecular ties. In all of these areas, capitalism has an immense capacity for recuperation and the production of seductions. For me, molecular revolution is not the addition of local micro-evolutions or micro-enterprises for local liberation. It involves taking into account an analytical dimension, the unconscious deformation of the entire social field, and unifying modes of subjectivation.

Kogawa: This might be a foolish question: do you have an affirmative model of the collective in sexual relationships as opposed to the family?

Guattari: No, I have no recipe. If it appears, it will come in the form of an assemblage of transformational movements, but it does not make sense at the moment to search for the right model and then to subsequently apply it. No. At the end of the 19th century, socialists thought that they had to educate the public in order to force any change in society. It's an illusion of the same type that produces this way of thinking, so we must move beyond this sort of relation.

Kogawa: As for May '68, in the opening stages of this movement, you speak of "the connection of the multiplicity of molecular desires which catalyze experiments of forces on a large scale." But what about the '77 Autonomia movement in Italy? Do you think that the same thing happened in this movement as well?

Guattari: Italy, for the past ten years, has been like a sort of immense social laboratory in which we can see the appearance of certain lines, the mutational tendencies of capitalism. It's in Italy that we can see how the traditionally marginalized have been taken into a new context that completely changes their significance. Today, in Italy, there are four million people who work on the black market and this is, in fact, a very important economic factor that supports Italy's capacity for exportation. We have also seen the appearance of a new type of attitude with regard to work in Italy today, which always existed among those who did not want to work: the homeless, the marginal, the maladjusted. But now it extends to hundreds of thousands of young people who, in a certain way, refuse the existing model of labor, who refuse not only the type of production but also the type of relations of production and, even more, the commercial forms of relations that had been channelling the work force through trade unions and traditional politics. The difference between the French '68 and the Italian '77 is that in '68, in France, the working class had been immediately controlled and captured by the CGT (La Confédération Générale du Travaille). But in Italy a very significant part of the youth, not only students but also the working and urban youth – with categories that are very difficult to distinguish, since we are speaking about precarity and it's not completely clear if we can speak simply about students or workers – have constituted this new form of organization that we call Autonomia, this new vision of structuring social and labor struggles.

Kogawa: Antonio Negri tried to extract some radical possibilities from such trends?

Guattari: Of course. And I would like to use this opportunity to bring to light the fact that the arrest and imprisonment of Antonio Negri, who has been my friend since April '79, was based upon completely false accusations without any grounds. Why is his detention scandalous? Because there is no evidence whatsoever against him. His day in court will never arrive, as is the case with the majority of his Autonomia comrades who are imprisoned today. To put it simply, he was the first theorist – along with a few others – who tried to illuminate this situation, which right now is being explored and rediscovered by many people, by members of the Italian CGT like Bruno Trentin.

Kogawa: Last year, the New York Committee Against The Repression in Italy was organized by my friends and others. In other countries the same thing has happened. Strangely enough, however, no newspaper here mentioned this repression with the exception of my small articles. The situation with free radio in Italy is the same. How did you become involved in Radio Alice? I think your involvement has a close connection to your own strategy and analysis.

Guattari: For a number of years I have been connected to various segments within Italian Autonomia and, in particular, I was in contact with the comrades from Radio Alice who called me at the moment when the entire team had been imprisoned in Bologna, at the request of the Italian communist party. Following this, we ourselves developed a free radio service in France, which earned me a trial and many difficulties with the police. The movement has now become important because there were a number of unions and political groups who became interested in the development of free radio given the fact that, in France, the monopoly over radio and television was seen as extremely oppressive by many people. There are a number of groups who broadcast illegally, despite the monopoly.

Kogawa: What is the theoretical background of your commitment to the free radio movement?

Guattari: First of all, when I participate in something, I don't wait to uncover its theoretical necessity. Rather, I find myself "plunging into it" so to speak. At the moment, I believe the essential question of creation is the utilization by the masses of a medium such as radio. A radio station managed directly by young people, by workers, by women in struggle, etc., helps to establish a new kind of contact between activists and the wider population, a contact that is much more direct. At Radio Paris 80, with which I'm associated, we receive dozens of phone calls requesting that we broadcast live. It's there that we find an aspect of what I call the "transversal transmission of communication" because listening to someone speak directly on the radio is very different from writing an article or having any kind of written communication. Here we have not only the communication of information, but also the transmission of affects, of another kind of semiotics. In this sense, the utilization of free forms of television and video will also offer us new areas to consider.

Kogawa: In your thinking, you often choose terminology from mechanics. For example, terms like assemblage, encounter, and segmentarity between two elements. These are very effective in not falling into the notorious dualisms of subject/object and production/reproduction. Could you tell me how you have worked out your terminology and your style?

Guattari: It consists in a certain notion about how conceptual systems function which, we could say, is already present in our work and which, we would hope, will also be shared by those who read our writings. For us, concepts are never universal categories. Rather, they are useful tools for a particular field. One should absolutely not believe in the notion, which I find stupid, of an intrinsic and scientific quality of a concept or of a body of concepts. Take for example this word, which is very difficult to pronounce in French and which I suppose is also the case in Japanese: deterritorialization. I encountered this concept in anthropology, in ethnology, where it describes a certain kind of territorialized power that names, in some African tribes, the opposition between the chief of the land and other minor political systems, for example, different types of filiation. From there, we became interested in political systems for which there does not exist a single territorialization of power. And so, as soon as we coined the term deterritorialization, this word began to function in other fields and we realized that we could talk about deterritorialized religions, deterritorialized sentiments, and that there existed a general movement of deterritorialization in certain societies. It doesn't matter if others accept the concept. If the concept is put into practice in a proper field – for example, artists have really taken to this concept – then great. However, if it doesn't work, this doesn't pose a problem either; we can just as well conduct such research with other kinds of concepts. Above all, we will absolutely not pretend to believe in the universality of our concepts. For us, the concept of the dialectic or the concept of abstraction do not function in a satisfying manner. It's for this reason that we developed the concept of deterritorialization, but perhaps others can arrive at a result that suits them better, with more traditional concepts such as abstraction or the dialectic. On the concept of the machine, I can construct a similar development and explain why we thought that this term had to be used not only in its accepted definition as a technical machine, but also as a theoretical machine, as an aesthetic machine, a social machine, and an economic machine. This led us to invent what we call desiring machines, which represent a kind of integration of all the different ways to use the word machine. I should point out that biologists, for example, use the term *engineering* with regard to genetic coding.

Part II: October 24, 1980

Kogawa: Can you discuss your ideas on the mass media?

Guattari: It's through the recent contact I've had with my friends in Italian Autonomia that I've really begun to understand the importance of free radio, precisely as a means for the renewal of social struggles. Free radio permits the establishment of a much more direct contact between individuals and the means of expression.

Kogawa: This was after Radio Alice in Bologna?

Guattari: Yes, free radio in France began in '78-'79. One should really understand that free radio in France is more of a movement than an actual group of radio stations; it is a movement of ideas that gave rise to the actions of radio pirates. But, above all, it's an ensemble that employs various types of means. It goes against the installation of fixed and permanent radios, which are exposed to intervention by the police. For example, Radio Paris 80 consists of very small broadcasting stations all run by just a handful of people and sometimes at locations that are not even radio stations themselves, but are rather places in which some people have attended a concert, or a political event, and have decided to quickly broadcast from this location. Actually, there is also a movement that developed in a very powerful way; it's the movement of the Citizens Band (CB Radio). So there are very diverse means of action and, in fact, what interests us is not simply to construct large and recognized stations, but rather to see that the form of radio, as well as other media like video or television, is available as a new means of expression for everyone. And it's fantastic that this makes governments and labor organizations anxious. The government, perhaps, would be willing to compromise and authorize some decentralized, regional stations under the condition that they would be controlled by local officials or by someone deemed responsible in those cities. Since the events of '77 in Italy, the power structure has imagined free radio as a kind of social dynamite, which is absurd since radio is nothing more than a means of expression. It can play either a reactionary or a progressive role through its connections with actual social groups. Basically, the technological transformations of radio, such as the miniaturization of its means of broadcasting, can be compared to the evolution, for example, of the means of reproduction. It is not the means that are revolutionary, but rather the utilization that social groups can construct from these means. Therefore it seems absolutely legitimate to demand one's freedom to use these means. For example, in the Soviet Union, one could not make free use of duplications and photocopies. But one always objects, insincerely, by saying that the free flow of radio-waves risks disturbing communications with airplanes and ambulances, etc. But it's an argument in bad faith, first, because what we're primarily asking for is a means of broadcasting short-range and, second, because we're not hostile to a federation of free radio, or to technical controls, so long as they're not under any kind of political or institutional oversight.

Kogawa: What about sponsorship by the culture industry?

Guattari: The situation is very ambiguous because there are very, very large private interests, particularly the stations run by record producers as well as big advertising agencies, who would be in favor of free radio. It's for this reason that a group in which I participate, called the "federation of non-commercial free radio," has proclaimed its support for non-commercial radio. The question concerning the legislation of advertising is of another nature; it's not our aim to finance our radio services through advertising. We would like to finance our radio by listeners who donate money if they like the programs, similar to how it currently works in the United States.

Kogawa: At the moment, they are all illegal?

Guattari: Yes, of course, and I am facing trials. My son, who is a radio technician, is also facing trials, the confiscation of materials. We cannot keep the police off our backs, avoid arrests, confiscations, and fines.

Kogawa: Is the station working now?

Guattari: Yes, it's called Radio Paris 80.

Kogawa: How many hours is the program?

Guattari: It depends. During the holidays we took a break. But in general there are around ten hours of programming per day.

Kogawa: Would you tell me more about the programs?

Guattari: I can only speak about the radio program with which I am involved. But there are others that are very different. There is, for example, a radio program that broadcasts very late at night, and all night, and only music. But there are over a hundred programs.

Kogawa: In the US, many colleges and universities have their own stations but they are never subversive.

Guattari: In France, what forces radio to become subversive is the absurdity of the monopoly of state power. Without it, there would be nothing subversive about radio. That's clear. The people who are involved are not subversives. It's the fact that we're up against this monstrosity of state power, which pretends to have control over the Citizens Band. These things are ridiculous, as if they wanted to control the tape recorders and the photocopiers. Free radio in this sense is not revolutionary. It's the contradiction that makes certain problems appear.

Kogawa: What about the program in Paris?

Guattari: One part of the program consists in providing information about alternative groups as well as information that is given directly by people who have phoned in. In terms of information, we are not connected to a network of special news agencies such that we could create an alternative press. Rather, all the information we broadcast is discussed directly by those people who call in. There is also a lot of direct coverage of meetings, of musical groups. We also receive cassettes, some recordings that are created by bands that we circulate directly. An Italian friend, who was one of the founders of Radio Alice, offered a good definition of what free radio should be: Free radio is important because when a person turns on his radio and hears strange sounds – the microphone falling on the floor, guys who are in the middle of arguing, there is a kind of shock and he says "What! This is radio?!" – it's something completely different than the stereotypical voices and characters that simply conduct linguistic performances. It's a demystification, a radio you can make, I can make, I can speak through. And I don't have to be a celebrity to do so.

Kogawa: Did you also talk about schizoanalysis at the station?

Guattari: Not in those exact terms, but I think that the phenomenon of radio is something like a schizoanalysis of the mass media. We don't necessarily need to create a discourse on schizoanalysis; it's enough to make free radio.

Kogawa: Generally speaking, the conventional function of mass media is basically to centralize and homogenize everything. At what point did you find another function in your free radio movement? For instance, to decentralize and to diversify. Can you talk about these theoretical points?

Guattari: The question of free radio goes far beyond the simple democratization of information. With Gilles Deleuze I considered that, strictly speaking, there did not exist a national language at the level of the assemblage of desire. Rather, we put into question the very notion of a national language. National languages always correspond to national formations of power. In fact, we are always involved with a multitude of assemblages or, as I say, with "different semiotizations." Without pausing, we then spoke about a multitude of different languages, *minor languages*. Children, among themselves, don't speak the same language that they speak with their parents; the language that we speak domestically is different than our professional language; the language that we speak in the ghettos is different than what we speak at the university; the language that is spoken on television is not the same as what we speak in our everyday life; and the language of love is different than the language of literature, etc. Dictionaries, the academies, and the official media all function in such a way as to make us believe in a single language and in the general translatability between all languages. But linguists, for example in America, have demonstrated that Black English is a different language than "official" American English and certain linguists have even tried to show that women do not speak exactly the same language as men. So another form of media, instead of crushing the specificities of these different languages, would on the contrary offer them the freedom of expression. What is in question then is the respect and the means given to the singularities of desires that correspond to these particular languages. Therefore, the mass media can move in two directions: it can become self-unified, crushing, translatable over the entire world into the same languages and sentiments, the same behaviors; or, on the contrary, it can help to make sense of what language *is*, what behavior *is*, what the desire of a particular group *is*, of how such a group of children live, a group of homosexuals, of poets, scholars. Above all, it can help to communicate the singularities of desire.

Kogawa: Gilles Deleuze was interviewed by *Cahiers du Cinema* for the November 1976 issue, where he mentions you while speaking about Godard. He said something like this: Godard criticizes the present cinema system in which the audience must pay and suggests instead that the producer should pay the audience. Deleuze says that you already pointed out a similar thing in that a psychoanalyst should pay his or her patients.

Guattari: At a conference of the Freudian School, there was a very formal question about the problem of money and psychoanalysis. I said, after making the audience laugh, that since the psychoanalyst works and the patient also works, both of them should be paid. After this, the chairperson quickly stopped the discussion.

Kogawa: I think it's a very important point.

Guattari: Yes. The important point is that the societies in which we find ourselves – societies that we can call capitalistic and that equally concern the countries of the East and the West – only valorize a certain form of production. We should not, in my opinion, be satisfied with the Marxist division of exchange value and use value. Rather, I think that we must introduce two additional forms of value: "values of desire" as well as what I call "machinic values." And exchange values should reflect these values of desire and machinic values. Machinic values are values of creation, of invention. Today, a technological innovation or a scientific equation will take its value from the register of exchange values if it can be found useful in the immediate process of production. But there are also values of aesthetic and scientific creation that do not have an immediate effect on exchange values and which, for this reason, actually deserve to be financed. Machinic values and values of desire are things that should be aligned with exchange value in the same way as any other use values. For example, the work of women at home or the work of children at school. Maybe it's a utopian vision, but it's something that permits us to understand and critique the mode of capitalist valorization. It's a question of the objective of the social division of labor. The social division of labor always converges with the values of capitalism, but we can imagine that it can also converge with everyday life, the environment, the possibilities offered by values of desire, values of creation. This is an entirely different social objective. Capitalism has constructed its system of hierarchy, of social segregation, on the scarcity of produced goods. But machinic values and values of desire do not depend upon the scarcity of goods. We can thus imagine a society in which human activities would not be under the dictatorship of the economic values of scarcity and this is what I call the perspective of a "molecular revolution." To change the goals of the social objectives of work, the objectives of activities, all this is possible if the productive machine is sufficiently developed to eliminate scarcity, to eliminate the need for housing, etc. But today capitalism artificially produces and maintains scarcity by starving a certain segment of the planet. It's absurd. To sustain this, it produces scarcity, for example, the scarcity of the university. The whole world cannot go study, but why? And scarcity in the means of expression in the media, but why?

Kogawa: Do you intend to continue to commit yourself to the radio movement?

Guattari: Yes, especially now, whereas before we were in very small groups. Now, there is the Socialist Party, all kinds of leftist movements, the CGT, which defends free radio except for the fact that it closed down Radio Longwy because it felt threatened. At the moment, the phenomenon of radio has become a national problem. At Longwy, there were very large workers' strikes against the closure of steel mills and, for over a year and a half, they developed a radio station that was very powerful, a free and open radio, open to other unions, to other groups, which did not please the confederalist direction of the CGT. It's always the same problem, in the sense that we can find a certain structure of state centralism somewhere within the operations of organizations.

Part III: May 22, 1981

Kogawa: Last time when I interviewed you, I did not ask about your criticism of psychoanalysis because I thought at that time that specialists who heard your lectures and met you should have written about it. But it turned out that in fact no journals dealt with such topics. I suppose they were scared because in Japan, contrary to Europe and the US, Freudian psychoanalysis has just recently begun to be institutionalized. So your criticism was probably too early for the Japanese system. So I would like you to explain some basic points, especially about the difference between schizoanalysis and anti-psychoanalysis or radical therapy such as R.D. Laing's.

Guattari: I will try to answer very briefly and schematically. Freudian psychoanalysis, but also Lacanian psychoanalysis, which is to say structuralist psychoanalysis, are both based on questions of language and so, in some ways, they take into consideration all of the phenomena that escape the comprehension of classical psychology. They are also devoted to uncovering what we might call the new continent of subjectivity. Only, instead of exploring this new continent, they have been behaving somewhat like the explorers of the 18th and 19th centuries, that is, of the colonial period, who were not really interested in what actually took place on the African or American continents. Rather, they devoted their efforts to adapting the populations to European life and European capitalism. Psychoanalysts have done the same thing. They have been interested in dreams, slips, deferred acts, psychosis, child psychology, myths, etc., not to better understand the specific logics of these areas, but rather only to restore them all to a dominant form of reason, to a dominant mode of life, which is to say, a certain kind of relation, a certain kind of familial triangulation, a certain kind of interpretation of reality. Here is my critique: there is something that escapes the realities of our developed societies, something which does not want to be an international movement, a school, a technique that we learn in manuals, something that forces us to reflect upon real analytic forms in the manner in which they appear. Not spontaneously, because there is nothing spontaneous about them, but as they appear within the social groups that are confronted by these kinds of problematics. We have to then attempt to show that there is a problem of the unconscious in the social field and that this problem not only concerns the specialists, psychiatrists, and psychoanalysts, but also everyone who, for example, attempts to live their life in a community, in a school, or in an activist circle. All of these people are confronted by such problems of the unconscious. For example, when in your newspaper or activist group you have someone who poses as the leader and who alienates all of the others, when you have the chauvinist attitudes of men, attitudes of inhibition, anxiety, fear, etc. In all of these instances, you are being confronted directly by a psychological and even psychopathological matter. So what can be done? As some might say: "It's not our problem, we are militants, we are activists, we are teachers, and those kinds of questions are best left for psychiatrists and psychoanalysts." Schizoanalysis, on the other hand, would like to say: no, these problems are also yours and not only because of some idea of human solidarity, but also for reasons that are highly political. Because, if you do not take these problems into consideration, you will inevitably be creating a dogmatic form of politics, you will inevitably not understand the contemporary functions of capitalism, which above all is a producer of subjectivity, a manipulator of subjectivity through the mass media and through public facilities. And so you will continue to organize the class struggle as if it were still the 19th century but, in doing so, you will be incapable of understanding the social struggles of today. The social struggles happening today should be concerned with taking care of these problems of the subjective unconscious and all the manipulations of which it is the object.

Kogawa: Do you think that conventional psychoanalysis, or even radical psychoanalysis, cannot deal with micro class struggle?

Guattari: I actually think that all of the psycho-sociological techniques, all of the American techniques of gestalt therapy, all of the techniques of group psychoanalysis, and also the vast expansion of family therapy techniques, avoid the problems of the microsocial and the micropolitical. However, I must say that in current family therapies there exists what we call "network practices" that force them to pose these issues. And here you will find a practitioner who is at the same time a theorist, namely Mony Elkaim, a Belgian psychiatrist, who worked in the United States and who is now the coordinator of the International Psychiatry Network, who tries to demonstrate that we can have a form of family therapy that's compatible with community struggles and with the problems posed by actual institutions. It seems to be a very promising trend though it's still in its infancy. I myself have participated at various gatherings and at various conferences. But today it seems that most of these theories and techniques continue to pose a kind of division between the social field and the libidinal field. And it's even the big theorists like Reich or Marcuse who have continued to argue that, fundamentally, political economy and libidinal economy are not the same thing, not parts of the same register. As for myself, I argue on the contrary that political economy and libidinal economy maintain a constant interaction of relations, *rhizomatic* relations. The current evolution of mass media, of computerization, of telematicization continuously shows us that today production and labor are linked, without pausing over such questions concerning the production and manipulation of subjectivity. Today, labor tends to be completely mass mediatized, informatized, and telematized. And so the problems of subjectivation are posed within the same processes of production and therefore we cannot separate them.

Kogawa: Many people say that you advocate something like, "revolutionaries should take their model from the actions of the schizo-process."

Guattari: I think these are formulas that I would no longer reiterate. They are formulas of a specific era, put forth at a certain moment when it was really necessary to move away from psychoanalysis and Lacanianism, which at that time were very powerful. During this era I wrote *Anti-Oedipus* with Gilles Deleuze, and we wanted to say that psychoanalytical models were essentially models inherited from a certain conception of the family and the relative neuroses among family members. These are what we called the Oedipalization concepts. In opposition to this, we argued that there are yet other modes of functioning. There is a mode of functioning in primitive or pre-capitalist societies, there is also a mode of functioning among children before Oedipalization, there is a mode of functioning of psychotics, etc. Therefore, we said that psychotic processes exist, but the word "psychosis" seemed too close to psychiatry and so from then on we decided to say *schizo* instead. We argued that there are *schizo* processes that traverse society and not only through psychopathology, but also through invention and all of those situations in which one encounters a rupture with the dominant forms of signification. Critics were then quick to tell us: "Ah great, so you argue that schizophrenics are revolutionaries." We have never said that! Schizophrenics are poor, unfortunate people who are imprisoned in psychiatric hospitals. What we did say is that there exists a *schizo* process that one can find sometimes in schizophrenia, sometimes in childhood, sometimes in invention, and sometimes everywhere. That's it. But this expression has generated so much misunderstanding that I think it's better right now to just forget it.

Kogawa: In my understanding, the aim of molecular analysis is to liberate the "mad flows of desire" or "mad libidinal flows." But many readers mistake these notions for something lunatic or irrational.

Guattari: Your question is of the same nature as the previous one about *schizo* processes. What Gilles Deleuze and I have together called "desire" is not at all equivalent to what Freud called "instinct" or "libido." Indeed the term has changed its meaning in this regard. We are not saying there is an instinctual infrastructure that will become representative of instinct. Rather, we wrote that there are multiple modes of functioning for society, for machines, for all that surrounds us, and for life itself. There are modes of functioning, which are stratified, which return to an initial state, which depend on a sort of principle of continuity as Freud called it, and there are modes of functioning that I call "far from equilibrium," far from the stratified equilibriums, to borrow a phrase from Prigogine. For us, desire takes place whenever anterior equilibriums – of signification, of structure, of a situation – are broken and this break, instead of bringing about a catastrophe, opens up a proliferation, a creation, generating new kinds of possibilities. This is what we call "desire." Today, François Mitterand's accession to power will be experienced as a catastrophe by many people and as a black hole by the bourgeoisie: "What will become of us? France is lost." I think, on the contrary, that it will not be brilliant president Mitterand who will shoot brilliant formulas out of his head like a Mao Zedong spitfire. But there will be a proliferation of possibilities. This is what I call desire. There, where everything seemed impossible, something is created. What is love between a young man and a young woman? It is not at all the wish to possess partial objects, to take possession of a territory. It cannot be reduced to such a libidinal operation because it is first and foremost the fact that in a closed universe, in two closed universes, things appear that previously seemed impossible. It's because of the fact that these two people, who both are individually encircled in themselves, in their families, in their egos, begin to see something else appear, some other possibility. Perhaps this possibility will be closed off again, recovered, or taken over by the form of the couple, by marriage, etc. But with love there is truly something *other* that is possible for me than the life I'm leading. And it is precisely this, which drives sexuality, which drives the caresses, the conflicts, jealousy, whatever you want. But desire is first of all this activation of another world of possibilities. This is our problem with desire: it is the economy of the possible that emerges from a rupture in the economy of the "already-there," the economy of the stratified, the economy of repetition. So this economy of the possible is something that scares people because they think "it's not logical or rational." But it's extremely rational in the sense that physicists today speak about thermodynamics "far from equilibrium." What is in question with desire is creativity, a change in the system, a breaking-up of structures. And this is something that is not at all an anti-scientific matter. It could perhaps be a matter of another kind of analysis, which could be at the same time pragmatic, political, scientific, social. But we cannot classify it because there is no science of the possible; there is no science which can predict the new. And yet there is something quite rational in saying that not everything is possible, not everything can happen in any which way. I think it's just the opposite. What is irrational is to think that the present state of affairs should continue. This is what's irrational. To think that Japan and France will continue in their ways and that, in light of present determinations, future projections can be made; this is completely insane and irrational. What is much more serious is to try to reflect upon what prodigious changes the youth in Japan will embrace or what changes the hundreds of millions of young people who live in appalling misery will adopt. It is imagined that they will all stay like this, that they will remain in a state of total alienation, of world-wide famine. But it is much more rational to think that something will eventually take place. I cannot predict exactly what it will be, but I can predict that something will happen. Things cannot continue the way they are and we all need to help with this change, which is not written in the *Bible*, or in *Capital*, or in Mao's *Little Red Book*, or in the program of François Mitterand.

Kogawa: Please give me a brief explanation of multiplicity. I think you differentiate it in two ways: molecular multiplicity and molar multiplicity. Can we understand the concept of multiplicity as a group concept?

Guattari: Yes, but it's a concept we find in Leibniz and also in all of classical philosophy. It's not that Gilles Deleuze and I invented the concept of multiplicity. Our aim with multiplicity is to try to move away from the subject-object couple. This dualism flattens all of the multiplicities that are neither subject nor object. It's a radically materialist position, in the sense that we do not consider the perspective that humans have of the world as the sole metaphysical truth. From this position, there is something that very much precedes the subject-object division. So what becomes interesting is to understand how the point of view of subjectivation establishes itself – the subjectivation of reality – and then also how human assemblages, social assemblages take hold of this reality. These are important questions. Then, schematically, whenever there is a system of representation, a schema of signifiers, of detours by all the devices of communication, well, there is a referent position within this representation and it's the subject who capitalizes, who memorizes the information, the representations, and who subsequently organizes her relations, her world in terms of this capitalization. Nietzsche said that he had used processes of the worst cruelty to create a human memory and, well, let's say that this memory is itself social subjectivity and what I would call a "molar usage of multiplicities." For example: the incarnation of the despot, or Jesus Christ, or the representative of multiplicities. But you can see that, if we remain here, we fall into an impasse because the despot becomes completely impotent and the representation becomes an icon, something to merely contemplate, which is out of our grasp. It is only when there is another kind of process, another kind of usage – which I would call the "molecular usage of multiplicities" – that there is an act, there is an event, a transformation. And this register is what Gilles Deleuze and I call a "diagrammatic function," which is to say we oppose representation to diagrammatic expression. To understand it better, take for example a simple form of cybernetic enslavement. When you drive a car you are generally enslaved – in the cybernetic sense – to the functioning of the car, your reflexes, your perception. The signals you receive from the road allow you to function without thinking, without having a representation of what you should be doing. Perhaps in some cases, an unexpected signal restores your sense of consciousness. And here representation intervenes to change the feedback systems, the semiotic systems of enslavement. But the normal function is at the level of the molecular usage of multiplicities. There is no subject who says, "Felix, you have to take your hand and place it on the gear stick." It's only when you don't know how to drive that the teacher says, "Put your foot there, do this, do that." Or, if you become a psychotic, at the moment when trying to walk up a flight of stairs you say, "But do I have my foot in the right place, is my foot okay?" and, as a result, you fall down. Normally, when you walk, when you have some grace, when you dance, you are not in the process of thinking, you are not in the process of representing your foot. And so, these are the two types of functioning that we can distinguish. On the one hand, diagrammatic functioning, when you have signs that function without any mediation or representation by a subject and, on the other, representative functioning, when you have signs which function in reference to a code, in reference to representative icons, in reference to a signified. However, the same multiplicities are the objects of both types of usage. It's the same multiplicity of buttons, of organs, of road signs, which are themselves taken in a molar functioning: "What am I doing? Should I hit the brakes? Where am I?" During the natural function of driving, someone who knows very well how to drive while thinking of something else can dream and almost fall asleep. I almost fall asleep driving myself; I reflect a lot while I'm driving. A great pianist is someone who does not think about his fingers, who does not think about the notes. Rather, he thinks about his interpretation, he thinks about the creative essence of the work that he's interpreting. He does not think, "Pay attention! In three measures I have a very difficult interval." Those are only the pianists in school. However, it's all the same multiplicity of texts, of notes, of sounds, of modalities.

Kogawa: For me, one of the most difficult things to understand is your commitment to semiotics. It seems very complicated to me. Could you explain your interpretation of semiotics? You differentiate many types of semiotics, for example signifying, a-signifying, post-signifying, and mixed semiotics.

Guattari: Let's look at things in a very basic way. Take a structure, for example the structure of matter, of a rock. A crystalline structure creates forms that reproduce and these forms are created by the atoms themselves. We can thus say that form and substance are totally inherent to each other. This is the first level. With plant and animal life, the form is transmitted by codes, by lines of codes that are distinct chemical chains. That is to say, we have the metabolism of RNA chains that creates complex molecules and systems of reproduction. Here we have the autonomy of code. So you see that when we pass from structure to code, there is a separation, an autonomization in the mode of coding. When we adopt human behaviors, the use of tools, we have modes of transmission that do not depend upon the genetic code. We have forms of learning; we have memories that are processed through language, through technology. And here we find another separation, what I call semiotics. The difference between semiotics and codes is that semiotics uses systems of signs, for example, in a totally linear way with reference to systems of interpretation whereas a code itself is not necessarily linear. The functioning of a code, the syntax of a code, participates in a mode of encoding. And here we can find the distinction between what Chomsky calls a syntax and the manipulated elements of this syntax: content and expression. This is because both expression and content in the genetic code are themselves tied together. The autonomization of syntax is what I call a machine of signs. Only there are many kinds of machines of signs: musical machines of signs are not the same as technological machines of signs used to do equations or chemistry. And these are not the same machines of signs that are used to pay exchanges, to make money. In certain cases, we have machines of signs that function without producing the phenomenon known as signification, for example, with money, with algebraic equations, with music. There may be significations, but only alongside. There's the semiotic text of Beethoven's music and there's also … oh, this reminds me of the Pastoral Symphony, this makes me think of little birds. But when you think of little birds in the Pastoral Symphony, this is not actually written in the text, this is not within the semiotic. The semiotic itself is a-signifying. Equations are there to help you build a bridge, but the equations themselves do not build bridges. It's the application that provides the signification, but algebra is a-signifying. And then you have human language, which mixes the a-signifying links, the phonemes, the lexemes, etc., with significations. However, the signifying semiotics that

I oppose to a-signifying semiotics are, at the same time, another kind of operation. It's an operation of power; it's a way of constructing a machine of power, of taking control over all the other codes, all the other semiotics. You have to think like the emperor does, like the despot. If you don't think like the despot, your way of thinking must adapt, it must become compatible with the dominant forms of signifying and encoding. All of the singular significations have to fold into and adapt to the dominant significations. These are the semiotic signifiers that always involve the establishment of formations of power, which is of critical importance in the history of societies and religions. Because the political and economic powers would be inconceivable without the religious powers, which interpret how the various forms of power should be articulated. How to articulate the fact that you are a child of a certain age, a man, a woman. How to interpret the passages, the initiations from one system to another? You produce for God, for the despot, for yourself, for your family. All this is made possible by an economic and political plan, which, because it's a machine that interprets significations, is from the outset a religious machine.

Kogawa: In short, your semiology mainly deals with the machinic unconscious?

Guattari: Yes, because with signifying semiotics we are always dealing with the social and with power. But with a-signifying semiotics we are dealing with the truth of things themselves. Signs encoded by a computer or informatics work directly, in the same way as physical-chemical processes and technological assemblages of machines, etc. We therefore have a kind of double description, in the sense that Marx described the relations and forces of production. The relations of production are always prisoners of signifying semiotics and productive forces always have something to do with a-signifying semiotics. However, the articulation of the two depends precisely on the processing of the machinic unconscious. The unconscious is, in this regard, both machinic and anthropological.

Butoh

Min Tanaka
the heir of darkness
his Zen fires burning beneath the feet of the Japanese miracle
in other districts of sense
a body-without-organs
beneath industrial identities
beyond narrative programs
slownesses in the speed of light
animal horizontalities
extracting his dances from the cosmos
diagrams of intensities
at the intersection of all the scenes of the possible
choreography of desire's dice throw
on a continuous line since birth
becoming irreversible of rhythms and refrains of a
haiku-event
I dance not in the place but I dance the place
Min Tanaka
the body weather
the naked king of our impossible memories of being

Body-Assemblage: Félix Guattari and Min Tanaka in Conversation

1. Threshold Phenomena

Félix Guattari: To begin, do you have any criteria with regard to a threshold or index that acknowledges, in a certain sense, you are becoming a marionette with regard to the passage in space of your flesh and skin? Does anything like a point of pleasure really exist, although I have no idea what to call it?

Min Tanaka: Marionette, that's a puppet, isn't it? Primarily what is at stake for a dancer, I think, is facing the gate of expression, that is, the question of what you are dancing. It is a matter related to this idea of becoming-doll. By affirming the principle that any expression exists in relation to the self (I), we can observe that the experiment performed by the dancer Min Tanaka consists in entering into an unquestionable inquiry. One might say that in relying on footwork in order to be more than what I am in the series of problematics that is Min Tanaka, I am trying to kick out of what will be in an instant outmoded. You mentioned flesh, could you explain this more concretely?

Guattari: Well, it's kind of like making mayonnaise. Sometimes it fails. Min san, have you ever sensed a threshold or sign that you have overcome something and in doing so changed the constellation of the universe? This would be a situation in which you come to despise your position inside your own coordinates, and then say to yourself: "oh, I did it, I overcame it!?" Another way to put this is, what is a lived experience of discontinuity?

Tanaka: An overcoming occurs in the site and in relation to it. What is my point of threshold? What does it mean to be a dancer on a public stage? Everything is getting vague. But just because I am constantly taking into account that I am overcoming a threshold, is this a cartographic initiative, an attempt at localizing myself within an environment? Or am I realizing that I am an environment as such? I can understand what you refer to as a certain sense of threshold or sign, precisely because the expression itself means projecting an arrow toward the abstract of an everyday that is not yet generated. It is this sense that is like crossing a border or traversing a valley. But is it about sense? In my case it seems to be connected to an idea of justice, duty or obligation. Even during a lived experience of discontinuity, if my condition is good, I can live without much consideration; but, if it is worse, I have to strive to think profoundly.

Guattari: In order to not state that I am thinking, I would invoke indexes.

Tanaka: I understand. But I think one doesn't have to call forth an index. I am always thinking without any pauses. But, I think I wish to become an agency that no longer has to think. Let me define myself as a being whose life is characterized by discontinuity.

2. On Horizontality

Guattari: I would like to posit two questions. One is specific, while the other is very general. As for the former, when you reach this dimension of horizontality – when you are creeping on the ground – is this somehow connected with a "becoming-animal?" Is there anything like a shift away from an anthropocentric perspective? This is my first question.

My second question relates to your animal becomings, or fluctuation of the universe's constellation. Have you ever collaborated with audiences which exist in a complex and refined state? Here I am thinking more broadly of audiences whose relations to phenomena were refined by the ultimate peak of poetry in Japan and China, Haiku, or paintings of traditional landscapes. Because there is an elaborate sophistication here, one that also existed in the mythology specific to the students during May '68, and which posits itself as the opposite pole in an oppressive relationship.

Translator: Can this be put differently at the molecular level…?

Guattari: Yes, is this on the molecular level or is there something that is highly elaborated and objectified, even in paradoxical form? It is thus aimed at activities belonging to threshold phenomena. On the other hand, is there anything significant about the gap that appears in combining verticality and becoming-animal, which relates back to my first question?

Tanaka: That's a very difficult question. With regard to the horizontality you mentioned in your first question, when I decided to dance by myself, I started to do this by lying down. I questioned myself whether I could dance by lying down horizontally. I was also skeptical about the public's point of view, because people believe that by simply standing and moving freely the body generates a dance, and this seems to me very problematic. And I was wondering about whether they would call this dancing or not. When I actually creep or lie down within an environment, what do they call me? It takes a lot of time to pursue questions about how I might resolve all these pressures from my surroundings and then bring my body to the next action; lying down on the street has changed my sense of audition and the appearance of humans.

I have been horizontal from the very beginning, and later decided to creep on the ground; this was a very deliberate decision. In other words, I felt as though I was raising myself from the horizontal. Additionally, since my childhood, I have had this habit of seeing the world from a terrestrial viewpoint. That is, I have this desire to set my eyes nearest to the ground. This was first a feeling and then a source of wisdom.

Guattari: Then are animals, or the animist dimension of your relation with the world, important for you? Have you ever had any significant dreams about animals?

Tanaka: I'm not so sure whether this is important or not, but I used to dream of animals, but recently this has diminished as I've dreamt mostly of humans, for dreaming is found in everyday life. Rather I let this go without forgetting about it. I've gone to the zoo quite often, but have never mimicked animals. I've attempted to pour animals into my body, wanting to encounter an animal living inside of me.

Guattari: This is exactly the point that I have been meaning to ask you.

Tanaka: On the issue of "animal becomings," a center or class is determined from the beginning, a situation with which I would not be satisfied. "Becoming" something is totally insufficient. It would be better to be frightened so that I could analyze it. Although both the vertical and horizontal are crucial levels to envision a society and look through the self, I am uncomfortable when they become a standard way to keep my balance. It would be better to be slanted, and, if objects cannot be so, then I can lean. Since childhood my eyes have been pointed in the direction of the vertical, so my perspective is always fluctuating, to the extent that something like this becoming ever happens.

3. On the Materials of Dance

Translator: What impressed me was what Min-san said about imagining the wind during the first "pushing discussion."

Guattari: The same holds true with me. But, how can I put it, is there anything more deterritorialized? For example, is the glittering of raindrops on the surface of macadam pavement not significant for you? Does this not enter into your workshop? Have you ever tried to "make an odor dance?" This fragrance is specific to some hour in the late afternoon, and it is what I would call a hypercomplex object.

Tanaka: Well, I don't fix any materials. They can be water or soil; or plants just as well. It is better to grasp materials in a bodily sense, which I call *winds* in my workshop, because they subsist as a kind of "common sense." That is why the object is never fixed.

Guattari: But is it done through deterritorialized components? Don't you use different, trans-semiotic elements, for instance, smells, sounds or impressions?

Translator: In this case, the point of view should be changed a little bit, even while retaining the same words and elements. When Min-san talks about wind, it is already made up of very complicated components. When a body is compressed by wind, if I can relate it to the question raised by Mr. Guattari, for instance, a case where, unlike addressing the rain in a Haiku poem, it is already so formalized that it has a complicated relationship that cannot be reduced to an abundance of significance. In other words, the body is not semantic.

Guattari: And then, one comes to the issue of site.

Tanaka: It is a question whether we call all space a site or have the materials required to be called a site. The rain is rain. The wind is wind. But they require movement. When one addresses the wind in a Haiku poem, it is no doubt that it is wind, no matter how one may express it. But we read wind precisely because the materials inside us and our bodies are moving. When I used the term "common sense" I didn't intend it to be taken in an infinite extension, but as a word for willfully regressing into myself, a point which is never something that represents reality. Wind is known either as a movement that demands perpetual stoppages or another in which we lose motivation. It also can be a wind that indicates the body is non-semantic. That is, the materials of both the site and the inside often coincide with one another. What is at stake, I think, is inherently found within the materials of myself, but at the same time, can be found outside of myself.

Consider the hypercomplex object mentioned earlier. Is there something about it that would prevent one from understanding another's pain, and that would be also deeply concerned with the topic of site? When we are talking about impressions, the basis is language. Rather, isn't the point that, before and after these impressions, one becomes a body or the inside?

4. Assemblage

Guattari: By the way, I would like to present the layered structure as follows: a theatrical space that is also a world consisting of intensities of the body. As the latter sometimes collides with the former, how do we control these layers and what sanctions float within them?

Tanaka: It may take a long time to explain this point because what is determining these layers is not me but an agency outside myself....

Guattari: That is exactly right. I am calling it an assemblage, which is collective. The collective assemblage does not imply the involvement of many people as it is an inhuman process. This inhuman process is a cosmic entity or a biological-hormonal history of abstract machines, and at the same time, can also be a history of rhythm imposed by a pure type of repetition that cannot be controlled by the logic of humanism.

Translator: In fact, Min's work consists precisely in detaching from this manipulative idea of assemblage.

Guattari: Beyond an individual assemblage....

Tanaka: It seems like a big mistake to treat something as if it were about my own event, given that an event happens outside me. For many years, I have believed that there would be no "my" time until the end of my life. However, I would never intend to live for the sake of others. I'm living for myself but I am nothing, for I wish to be thoroughly more myself than anyone else. For example, nature had originally been dancing. Through observing its dance, our senses themselves dance; then they are raised to the level of intelligence. A long continuation of the human/inhuman process, I think, arranges our dancing. My point is to return to the outside and surface of the body.

5. On Improvisation

Translator: As is well known, an actor who improvises has to locate him/herself in freedom and necessity at once. There is a kind of threshold, which is neither posited distantly nor closely … a threshold where a coincidence emerges between distance and proximity.

Tanaka: Generally, freedom cannot be taken into account if some fiction precedes it. One has to adopt a perspective as an ensemble of thoughts, that is, an improvisation which always exists "between" them. One might misunderstand that playing more freely or anarchically is an improvisation, yet nothing proceeds well without recognizing what enables improvisation. Since improvisation has become one of the methods of artistic expression, it turns out not to have been a dream. It is just something like a pathway into a dream. Intuition comes from perspective. An intuition stands up in a single stroke, and then creates a fringe.

Translator: After all, this improvisation is an immediate creation and "written retention" of a moment.

Tanaka: I am the old Min Tanaka at each moment, taking note of retentions. It is more concrete to call improvisation a relentless dreaming rather than a direct creation. Licking clouds in the sky, or embracing the shadow of fish in a glance upon the surface of a river; shouting "truly delicious!" while enjoying meals. By listening closely to the words of an interlocutor, I try to make my brain turn over. An improvisation requires, whenever it may occur, whatever you may see, neither becoming stable nor proclaiming that it is new. I call this improvisation a *body-weather*.

6. On the Problem of Representation

Translator: We now turn to representation, because I think it is required by many artistic expressions, including theater. The issue here is in mounting something for theater audiences something else is imposed as the true question, that is, as the problematic that gives to drama the role of representation and realization, even if the reality at issue is complicated and multi-layered. After all, isn't it at the point in-between the representation and the realization that the true question is posed?

Guattari: It is incorrect to place these into an opposition. Let me clarify. I would divide these ideas into three categories; albeit there are, in fact, four categories, namely, the level of territorialization-deterritoralization, which I won't take into account here.

First, I situate an ensemble of materials belonging to discursive logic – let's call it a discursive ensemble – on the one hand, then conversely I locate the notion of the "body without organs" borrowed from Artaud on the other hand, which is non-discursive. On this pivot point there is the production of existence, on the left side, one encounters a representation – a substantial temporal-spatial body is given here – on the right side, there is no given substantial body (Guattari explains this by using the blackboard). Actually, I can translate the production of existence into a term of representation. There is always a translation. Then, for me, there are flows (fluxes). It is the discursive flow that is incorporated into the sensual and non-discursive territory, that is, a flow that is incorporated into the existential territory, yet wherein it turns back as a flow of expression. This constitutes a relation of representation or signification. This flow 1 (f1) is founded as a second flow 2 (f2) through the process that is mediated by the place producing this existence. Then, a further relation is generated between the first flow and the second, and a body is assembled where this relation becomes complicated….

Tanaka: Yes, absolutely yes, and it is very fast.

Guattari: But here one cannot see the problem of improvisation, which in my view is a special problem belonging to theater, because what exists there is a certain fixed level and presentation insofar as the same discursive or semiotic component transforms itself and entails creating another type of existential territory. Put differently, the gesture that carries a certain signification or message is enabled by something which produces its rhythm, contours ... and existential territory. At that time, theater is said to be a place where the mutation between discursive components occurs. The function of this place is deployed within other forms of semiotization in the regime of representation, and at the same time, produces a certain existential territory, which is deployed in a non-discursive register, and then makes theater flourish – the fact that there is a production of theater, and in the induction of a theater, the induced annihilates the inducing. However, an idea from theater is not only discursive.

Tanaka: When I use the expression "then it begins, from now it starts," it precisely coincides with this cycle and complication. The more its speed increases, the more I cannot help thinking so. Both representation and realization are simultaneous, especially when I am dancing in the best of conditions.

Keiichi Tahara's Faciality Machine

What is a photographic portrait? The impression of a face taken so as to produce a representation, but also the borrowing of certain traits of this face for completely different ends, such as the denotation of a proper name, the evocation of a memory, the triggering of an Affect.... It is on this second aspect of the portrait that Keiichi Tahara primarily works. In fact, he only retains, from his "subjects," the traits that he can use to prepare the landscapes that obsess him and, above all, so as to obtain a certain effect of subjectivation, toward which his oeuvre as a whole tends. What is it a matter of? Of a transfer of enunciation: instead of it being you, the spectator, who contemplates the photograph, it is suddenly the photograph that surprises you, which starts to scrutinize you, which interpellates you, penetrates you right to the soul.

By means of the hundred or so photographs of personalities collected in the present album,[1] it is possible to take apart the Taharian machine that brings about this effect. It essentially comprises three components that we will examine in succession:

---

1. Presentation for a collection of portraits by the Japanese photographer Keiichi Tahara, *Keiichi Tahara* (Paris, Audiovisuel, 1991). In the presentation of this text for *Cartographies Schizoanalytiques* Guattari footnotes the many portraits he is referring to by proper name. Here a footnoted name is provided only if it is not clear from the context to whom Guattari is referring. [TN]

- a deterritorializing cutting out of the face
- a fractal rupture of the gaze
- the attaching of an original proliferation of significations – which thus find themselves attached to the proper name – to this apparatus

Considered without any particular aesthetic qualification, the human face already originates in the detaching of a gestalt figure from an animal muzzle as ground. A face, which is culturally acceptable, is thus obliged to bend to the typical intervals of authorized significant movements (for example, a smile that exceeds a certain threshold of size would refer to the grimacing of an autistic person or a moron.) However, Keiichi Tahara endeavors to work the traits of faciality in registers of framing and lighting effects that would bring them out of these pre-established montages of signification and would reveal original potentialities. Thus, the faces to which he is attached will find themselves carried off toward non-human, animal, vegetable, mineral, cosmic becomings of abstract composition ... that are constitutive of what one might call prospective unconscious dimensions.

This play of framing can proceed at a general level. In contrast to the general frame of the photo, which finds its angles systematically rounded off in an effect of fuzzification, this type of internal reframing can be carried out by way of a window[2] or even a mirror.[3] It can equally be done by the implanting of frames that are lateral to the face or to the person and it then consists in a tableau,[4] in quadrangular objects[5] or even in a rectangle of light hanging over the scene.[6] The combinations of the two procedures are frequent. For example, the window at which Boltanski appears itself encompasses other windows and these three stages of fractalization by the nesting of frames then find themselves prolonged by the multitude of layers and branches that seem to envelop the person represented in American shot.[7] This fractalization of

2. Christian Boltanski or Philippe Sollers.
3. Roy Lichtenstein or Laura Betti.
4. Bernard Lamarche-Vadel, Pierre Klossowski.
5. Tadeus Kantor.
6. Iannis Xenakis or Mario Merz.
7. "Plan americain" is a term from French film criticism that refers to a framing of a character in three-quarter length, medium-long shot. [TN]

framing can sometimes result in a generalized disruption.[8] On other occasions, as is the case with Bram van Velde, it leads, inversely, to a static putting into perspective, conferring on the person a sort of stamp of petrification and eternity. In more than half the portraits, the play of light operates by a vertical cut that bars the face with a fractal line of shadow. The most typical case in this regard is doubtless the portrait of Ricardo Bofill, which opens the collection. In effect, all that subsists of his face is a narrow vertical strip that represents barely a quarter of the photograph's surface, while the left eyebrow, the eye, a transverse wrinkle and the corner of his mouth comprise the luminous mass that remains. When the vertical cut is external to the face,[9] and equally when it stays at a tangent to it,[10] the cut stays in the form of a straight line. In the case of Buren, it finds itself multiplied like a series of … columns! It is much rarer for the luminous cut to be horizontal. However, that is the case with Iannis Xenakis, when it brings to mind a musical score cut vertically by a stave. Let us note, with Maurice Rheims a different form of horizontal and vertical crossover and a similar crosscutting with François Truffaut, to which a pure and simple detachment of the head is added.

Another rather frequent method of deterritorialization of the face by the play of light consists in making a small part of it emerge from a large dark mass.[11] It is also worth signaling the use of blurring by the decentering of focal distance,[12] by local shifting[13] or by the use of cigarette smoke,[14] and distinguishing the blurred face in the foreground from general blurring.[15]

Considered for themselves, in their serial effect, or in association, the ensemble of these procedures of a deterritorializing cutting out prepares the ground for putting the second component to work, that for its part will no longer be content with merely fractalizing the spatial frame but the Assemblage of enunciation as well.

8. Daniel Buren, Lamarche-Vadel, Sollers, Iris Clert.
9. Louise Nevelson.
10. Joseph Beuys.
11. Alain Robbe-Grillet, Joseph Beuys, Brion Gysin, Christian de Posampac.
12. Jean Degottex, Iannis Kounelis.
13. Xenakis, William Burroughs.
14. Philippe Soupault and Romain Weingarten.
15. Jean Carzou and Roland Torpor.

From the first, decidedly prototypical, portrait of Ricardo Bofill, what seems to me to be the heart of Keiichi Tahara's aesthetic goal finds itself laid bare. To apprehend it, it is worth pinpointing the play of complementarity that is established between the visible eye of the left of his face and the invisible eye of the right of his face, which is ready to reappear in a fugitive but fulgurant, quasi-hallucinatory fashion, on the basis of the miniscule trace of white that remains of it. It is from this metonymic coming and going that the existential effect of being-seen-by-the-portrait originates, a theme that was dear to the Surrealists and which I have already evoked. We are now in a situation in which the ensemble of faciality traits has been destabilized by the deterritorializing treatment of lighting and framing. Henceforth, the structural key to the image no longer adheres to the "photographic referent" such as Roland Barthes defines it ("I call 'photographic referent' not the *optionally* real thing to which an image or a sign refers but the *necessarily* real thing which has been placed before the lens, without which there would be no photograph").[16] It finds itself transferred to the imaging intentionality of the spectator. My gaze finds itself "dragged into" the bringing into existence of Bofill, without it, his soul would be scattered to the four winds. But this appropriation turns back on me, sticks to me like a sucker. In its precariousness, this being-there sticks to my skin. It doesn't stop gazing at me from my interior. In short, I am bewitched, the evil eye is cast upon me, I am expropriated of my interiority.

The vis-à-vis of the photographs equally works at extracting an autonomous, abyssally fractalized gaze. A face-profile movement can be sketched out, a contrast of light, of posture ... all things that animate and hollow out representation. In this regard, two of the most significant portraits concern Arman, in which relations of complementarity are established between his beard in the left foreground and a sculpture made of metallic pincers in the right background, the half-lit face on the left and the black profile on the right, the eyes in shadow corresponding to the full opening of the eye-window protected by bars.

In addition, one ought to take stock of other modes of enactment of this same existential effect:

16. Roland Barthes, *Camera Obscura: Reflections on Photography,* trans. Richard Howard (New York: Farrar, Straus and Giroux, 1981), p. 77.

- The obscuring of the eyes of Maurice Rheims by means of a horizontal bar of shadow or his being completely back-lit
- The half-closed eyes of Mario Merz, on whose eyelids a glimmer of light appears, constituting a sort of second vision
- The reflection of the frames of the spectacles of Degottex, which are substituted for the brightness of his gaze
- The total vitrification of the blind gaze of Juliette Man Ray, the emission of a luminous cross from the lenses of Levi-Strauss' spectacles or the luminous effervescence of Maurice Rheims' eye
- The white of the eye which stands out on the face[17]
- Or, in a more frequent fashion, the iris,[18] or perhaps cornea,[19] that becomes the seat of the emission of a light-gaze

It is thus on the basis of a fracture of sense that this existential transfer of enunciation is set off, the portrait's capturing of the gaze. Roland Barthes had apprehended this phenomenon through the opposition he makes between the "studium: in which the signification of the photo is coded, and the 'punctum'" "sting, speck, cut, little hole – and also a cast of the dice ... that accident which pricks me."[20] He described the force of metonymic expansion of this point of rupture and established a difference between the punctum, founded on a "detail" that interferes in the register of forms and what he calls a stigmata punctum, which for its part intervenes in a harrowing domain of Time, its lacerating emphasis. But, for me, this stubbornness of facticity – "that-has-been" – with which the intentionality of the image collides is no more than a case (his meditation on the photograph of his dead mother, for example) that perpetuates a memory folded in on itself. Keiichi Tahara's portraits indicate another path for us, because his principal concern evidently resides neither in denoting the identity of his "subjects" nor in circumscribing the charges of signification of which they are the bearers. Certainly one sometimes finds references to the domain that confers their fame on them here, but always in the mode of indirect allusions.

17. Romain Weingarten.
18. Laura Betti, Adolphe Spier.
19. Philippe Soupault.
20. Barthes, *Camera Lucida*, p. 27.

Here their attested faciality no longer totalizes faciality traits. On the contrary, these start to interfere with contextual traits. They bring deterritorialized Universes of existential reference into existence. But, thinking about it, are we not in the presence of a general faciality function? The face of Christ, like the traces on the Turin Shroud, hasn't stopped haunting Western capitalistic subjectivity, like the faces of President Washington, Lincoln and Jackson on the American dollar! All signification is inhabited by a deterritorialized faciality that confers on it less its formal sense than its existential substance. What speaks to me as a sensible quality, as a gestalt, as an abstract problematic, always does so as an enunciative nucleus incarnated in a face (facialitarian reterritorialization). The voice itself finds itself pre-disposed by this kind of non-discursive faciality which imposes itself as the presence to itself of an absolutely different present. It is not a matter here of the presence of a "big Other" in the structuralist lineage of Lacan, but of an alterity modulated by the big and small turns of history and by the mutation of technological Phyla.

In this regard, to consider photography as a more or less surpassed step in a line that would progressively lead us to cinema, video, computer-assisted digital imaging, etc., would be an unfortunate misunderstanding. As Roland Barthes forcefully underlined, it is in the photograph, more than any other art form, that the existential temporality of the machines of representation lies. Most other media are too talkative, their narrative programs dominating enunciation too brutally, substituting for it, expropriating the free processes of subjectivation of which photography alone can allow the powers of partial temporalization to be deployed (with the exception of the comic strip perhaps, which is capable of equalling it on this terrain).

The very particular interest of Keiichi Tahara's work, in the lineage of his greatest predecessors, consists in diversifying and making the maximum play of what I will call the machinic components of the "armed" gaze. One meets again here, in new modalities, this sort of subjective effacing of the photographer that Moholy-Nagy sought and which led him, more than half a century ago, to distinguish the production of eight types of gaze: abstract, exact, rapid, slow, intensified, penetrative, simultaneous and distorted.[21] This sort of deterritorializing and de-subjectifying treatment of the portrait consists in staging, in "landscapifying" a processual faciality on the basis of traits that are offered passively to the enunciator. Once again, let us consider some examples.

In the portrait of Kounelis, two discs of raw light break away from the eyes, literally tearing the gaze toward us. They echo an equally rounded glimmer of light that doubles the right-hand side of the face like a collapsed halo. Consequently it is the whole photograph that becomes an eye, the head itself being nothing more than a bulging pupil. The molecular mystery of Arman, where it is a white globule that is parasitic on his nostril and resonates with other circles and white traces behind his head, in counterpoint to the absent eye, on the one hand, and on the other, with the photo facing him, the sculpture of metallic pincers. In the case of Buren, the two white globules have become two conspicuously overexposed white shirt buttons, vibrating with a population of large-headed pins that become thorns on a map of Europe folded into a Chinese screen. Two large lampshades have taken the place of eyes in the portrait of Philippe Sollers and this time the punctum has been displaced to the edge of the tableau, in a way that makes one think of a painting by Jasper Johns, with its stencilled numerals and letters. And finally Robbe-Grillet, where, this time it is two cuneiform signs of light that mark the bottom of the photo, like two space capsules starting out on their umpteenth trajectory. (The previous works of Keiichi Tahara already frequently had recourse to this type of "parasiting," including through the use of reflections in glass frames.)

Keiichi said to me one day "I first have to understand through the gaze, even when I don't take a photo. Then the impression stays in my head and there's no longer any difficulty…." To understand here is to free oneself from the superimposed significations that are imposed on the facialitarian landscape as if by themselves, it is to allow oneself to be dominated by the other gazes that organize themselves before your eyes. The importance of the multiple fractal cracks engendered by the photographic apparatus as conceived by Keiichi Tahara resides in the fact that,

---

21. Cited by Susan Sontag, *On Photography* (New York: Farrar, Strauss and Giroux, 1973), p. 122.

leaving certain interpretative sequences yawning, it leads these latter to reiterate themselves emptily, indefinitely, and to secrete new existential stases, accompanied by new lines of sense and new Universes of reference. The partial nuclei of enunciation and existential taking body that thus find themselves established enter into transverse correspondence with part objects (in the sense that Freudians gave to this term) and connect the scopic drive to a Constellation of other spheres of interest and desire. The proper names that Keiichi Tahara brings us to apprehend from an unforeseen angle then become the notes of a musicality that everywhere exceeds them. It is no longer a question, I repeat, of denoting an identity or of connoting a message. We are no longer in the register of identifications and mediatized communications. It is by immediate transference without any hesitation that these deterritorialized bodies are given to us, without limit and without organs, constituting so many effects indexed simply through their proper names.

© Keiichi Tahara

© Keiichi Tahara

© Keiichi Tahara

The "always never seen"
of Keiichi Tahara

There are already so many things, words, people fluttering in all directions! How to navigate? For his part, Keiichi Tahara has decided to focus his psychic sensibility and photographic perception on just one. But, so that all is not caught up in mute fascination, he chooses this ultimate thing, which is vibrating, fluctuating on the verge of the melting point, where it can take on an unforeseeable power of proliferation. And to compose a groping gaze, to locate the edges of a nascent world, he must perform a radical deframing of the photographic act, by relinquishing the old ideal of objective denotation and by refocusing on the mutations of visual enunciation that result from his "weapons" of the most sophisticated technical means.

Paradoxically the "never seen," which is thereby revealed, fits perfectly with the "already seen" of the most archaic, the most archetypal, such that we can speak of a machinic or machined subjectivity produced by this complex *dispositif*, which is the most intimate that can be sensed without ever becoming familiar. Because there is no fixed orientation, because there is the wandering like a dead soul that the mourning rituals have not yet appeased.... Threatening by its arbitrary yet necessary burden, reassuring by its stowing the most assured evidence. Yes! It's a window, it's a radiator, it's a guy with glasses wearing a round cap.... From what visual effects can we identify this turning-upon-itself of Keiichi Tahara's objective and this new primacy of enunciation?

First of all, those of its outermost presentation: we have the shadows cast by the frames as a result of their angle of arrangement on the walls of the exhibition space as well as the abrupt reflections of the supporting glass; and the rhythmic choices determining their spatial layout according to multiple temporalities; in short, an entirely ephemeral art, familiar to the Orient, which makes incorporeal crystals manifest; the iconic content subsisting, for a time, only as existential pretexts. Then, as a disharmonious counterpoint, we have the intrusion of surface singularities – scratches, rubbings, streaks, various impressions – inherited from the techniques of painting today. (I surprised myself by wanting to erase, tissue in hand, some traces embedded in a print that in fact remain as a technical purity without equal!)

For its part, the internal framing has been designed to generate a permanent instability of the relations between figure and ground. The primary modules of semiotization thus find themselves in a condition that allows percepts and affects to work, so to speak, of their own accord. Rather than the Freudian "primary process" of dreams – too much at the mercy of blowback from "secondary elaboration" – I'm thinking here about the "functional phenomena" specific to the crepuscular states described by Herbert Silberer or the "primary delusional experiences" identified by Karl Jaspers that accompany what is commonly called "delusional flashes." But don't misunderstand me. It's not at all a question of comparing these photographs to the images of projective tests like the Rorschach, whose obsessive symmetries program an irremediable subjective closure. As machines that undo the common sense of forms, Keiichi Tahara's diagrams throw us, on the contrary, into a universe without foreseeable ends, without the delimitations of identity. The scenes of heterogeneous enunciation are determined by singular matters, of which no structural paradigm can deliver the key. Chords of unheard-of-senses are deployed by harmonies and dissonances that are not accountable to any principle of contradiction or sufficient reason. A piece of Montblanc silver paper ignites on contact with a frame leaning against the corner of the wall.... A comet at twilight passes through an ether of granular sensuality.... A tropical explorer – again the guy with the round cap – hovers between parquet floorboards and a forest of domestic sequoias.... A pane of glass explodes into kanji gesticulations then solidifies as a futuristic Zen temple.... A *Victory of Samothrace* – still in silver paper – is poised to jump out the window.... An abstract of Mondrian, who had been dozing since the dawn of time above the radiator, awakens to a greenhouse effect worthy of Vuillard or Bonnard.... The ego, the I, the other, and everything else subsequently cascade down into a dark aquarium in which the impassive eye of an Egyptian fish is enthroned....

Imai: Painter of Chaosmosis

Chaotic plunge into matter, osmosis between a gesture of abolition and complexity regained. From his period of gestural abstraction to his *Ka-cho-fu-getsu* ("Flowers-Birds-Wind-Moon") turn, Imai has affirmed himself as a painter of chaosmosis.

Chaosmosis of the immediate, sensual, sexual, gesture that seizes the canvas. Chaosmosis of the mute expectation of "dripping," which evokes the performance of traditional Chinese painting when the watercolor vigorously reaches the delimitation of *tache*-territory. Chaosmosis of the personal trajectory from childhood in the refined milieu of Kyoto; to the solitude, cold, and hunger of Montparnasse in the 50s; to the cosmopolitan nomadism around the world mixed with an ambivalent anchor in Japan during its frenzied modernity of the 70s; until the emergence, within the texture of his work, of iconic refrains that led to his being dismissed by many critics who had previously revered him.

So, in short, the cycle of the hero in postmodernity! But not Imai! No! As some had predicted, his work would buckle neither from a resigned acceptance of traditional values nor from an abandonment of subjectivity in the mass media marketplace! The proof is that the drippings from the crazy countercultural years became superimposed onto the clean figures of the first *Ka-cho-fu-getsu* in order to distort, pollute, *denature*, these figures beyond the frame, emancipating themselves, deploying hyper-cubic dimensions, catalyzing horizons of false perspective and "strange attractors." Behind the Imai acknowledged by the establishment always looms the bad boy of the Beat Generation, of Action Painting and Happenings. Thus, Imai constituted himself at the interface of several generations of painters and several figures of contemporary artistic sensibility.

To the repetition of embossing, the dissemination of prefabricated units, responds the torrential character of his production, which prides itself on more than 200 paintings each year. All stages of his work are marked by the physical pervasiveness of his gesture of appropriation of the canvas. No bravado, no narcissism here but rather fierce affirmation of existential resistance. A thousand depressive traps await the painters of our time. Toshimitsu Imai, although no exception to the race toward the abyss that characterizes modern art, intends to survive. Blindfolded, the Imai-enunciation finds its way among formalist glaciers, hyperreal catatonia, and conceptual reefs. Sexually obsessed erection, conjuring the fear of falling: each work is a unique resurrection of the body, of the earth, of the world of art. "Yes, here I am, still here!" despite the threats, curses, and easy seductions. Or rather because of them. The dizziness of forgetfulness, of non-sense, of the simple banality that masters its energy by retaining gesture. Pictorial ritual. Song of the world. Acquired certainty that, through a mad gesture, the emergence of a minute bifurcation will cause a repetition. Clinamen. There, between informal evanescence and conceptual abolition, Imai's refrain, reminiscent of a wallpaper pattern, a screen, a fan, a kimono, catalyzes the worlds of childhood, worlds we once knew, but also new worlds never before seen through the cracks of *déjà vu*.

A refrain like a swirling flower on an aleatory ocean; a refrain that reemerges as a strangely familiar attractor. What Imai explores here is the possibility of a flash concatenation between chaos and complexity, which has no obligation to exhaust itself in the alternative of All or Nothing. Imai's brush hovers somewhere between being and nothingness, at a point where they embrace each other in order to create mutant intensities. Ontological invagination by heterogenesis. Representation implodes, is diverted toward worlds where there is never a question of distinct oppositions, of Manichean valorization. Immobile vibration of an a-typical, a-topical, a-chronic enunciation, hanging on the tip of an eyelash, on the wing of a butterfly, thrown into the wild java of a summer dust cloud, in the basement at a time when the bottle rack had not yet been "collectivized" by Marcel Duchamp, *et al.*

Flowers-Birds-Wind-Moon: an initiatory refrain, an event always already there. Put your gaze on hold. "Keep cool, take it easy." Never was this becoming-Japanese in line with tradition, despite perverse appearances. It was labored by the China of yesterday and tomorrow, by Korea, the U.S.A., by the islands of the south. Its incorporeal and ancestral worlds are coupled with the most deterritorialized machines. Imai remains fundamentally Japanese because he constantly betrays Japan. This is a child, a sage, an insect forever occupied with the reiteration of its mark, its imprint, its ritual of existential appropriation. A little night music in the wax museum of *Blade Runner*. Breathless and yet the gaze imposes itself. The peaceful fixity of Imai's world comes down to its expansion at infinite speed. Total work, open work. Because, just as much as the gestures and impressions from tradition, we find the repugnance of the well-informed art critic and the mixed acquiescence of Japanese political correctness: "Are all these drippings really necessary?"

Conceptually, Imai painted using subjective putty with an eye toward a "public good" he knew how to tame. No cynicism here, no deception. Or maybe an essential deception, one holding the contradiction at its melting point. No, just the air of time on the palette. So goes the world. So good, so sweet. Becoming-bamboo-shoot in a large park, Sunday morning, to the sound of rock music. Becoming a cheap flowers-birds-wind-moon toward an imperceptible density of being. To go faster than the chaosmic wind, to open the cosmonaut eye-moon, to make of bird song as-yet-unheard-of digitized refrains.

The Rich Affects of
Madam Yayoi Kusama

At some point a long time ago Yayoi Kusama broke through the invisible wall of the quotidian that generally prevents our exploration of the germinal state of the world. This ordeal led her neither to a narcissistic mortification nor autistic in-folding; instead, she conferred on it the singular power of guiding us toward the explorations of vegetal and vegetative virtualities which haunt our subjectivity. From then on any misinterpretations that relate the genesis of her work to a repression or an infantile fixation, as Freudian analysts would certainly not fail to point out, do not allow us access to the world she offers, and which is not at all reducible to the composition of elementary drives or to a montage of structural patterns. Kusama decomposes matter, form, color and signification up to a necessary and sufficient point from which she can then recompose vectors of sensibility and meaning with a much greater scope than those with which she initially began. In this respect her creative movement shares certain similarities with chemistry. She sets out on the path of indifferentiation and of modular proliferation that at best leads us, subsequently, down a path of highly elaborated and differentiated processes. She is committed to producing what I call hypercomplex affects. It is surely a false and pernicious idea, which has ravaged the human sciences, to represent affects as species of raw matter and undifferentiated energy. Rather, affects are variable matter-flows that, while indexed only to a non-discursive domain, are not as a result any less of a bearer of infinitely rich potentialities.

Thus, the intensities engendered by Kusama's compositions, while remaining anchored in a very traditional Japanese imaginary, above all constitute extraordinary dispositifs of subjectivation and aesthetics of the most modern of materials, those which, let's not forget, our societies of consumption otherwise reserve for their miserable and disenchanted universes. This woman, who blazed across – but at what cost! – the creative-destructive years of the "Beat Generation," is reborn under our eyes as a great contemporary artist forging the sensibility of a most unpredictable future.

The Architectural Machines of Shin Takamatsu

The history of contemporary Japanese architecture is one of a progressive disengagement from International Style, with its white and abstract rectangular forms, its pilotis, its flat roofs, its plain facades or glass surfaces, as well as of a reconversion by way of resingularization. This history is punctuated by upheavals brought about by two key figures whose names are Kenzo Tange and Arata Isozaki.

In the sixties, Kenzo Tange made a radical rupture with the simplistic aspects of international functionalism by establishing a structuralist movement in Japanese architecture and urbanism. Contrary to this structuralism, which emphasized the complexity of relational aspects of architectural spaces, a movement called "metabolism" developed that attempted to adapt the new industrialization of buildings to human needs, in particular the building of agglomerations of modular capsules. With a similar concern for taking into account societal specificities, both individual and cultural, the metabolists were also very interested in composing forms that evoked traditional Japanese structures or relating itself to them indirectly. Aside from Kenzo Tange, there was his student Arata Isozaki who also sought to radically disengage Japanese architecture from modernist classicism in order to pave the way for a symbolist and mannerist creativity that sometimes bordered on surrealism.

Today these upheavals, together with the economic vitality of Japanese society, have resulted in an exceptional effervescence of architectural production. Applying the label "new wave" to the most inventive architects of the current generation is quite arbitrary given that their diversity is so huge. But it would be even more imprudent to group this generation under the banner of "postmodernism" since they have fortunately escaped the superficial and eclectic opportunism that generally applies to this qualification in the United States and Europe. However, what seems to traverse the pluralism of these Japanese creatives is what I call their processualism, which is to say precisely that they escape the pre-established modelizations of schools or movements. Not only have they each strived to develop their own personality; they have each followed the evolution and mutations that traverse their own processes of creation. By always refusing such systematic labeling we can identify, in these architects, some evolutionary becomings that develop very naturally by avoiding all functionalist frameworks, exigencies of context, or even humanist cultural references. At times they have been described as hermetic but such an opinion is badly formed, especially in Japan, where we have seen a resurgence of a will to singularization in this century.

From the assessment of contemporary Japanese architecture conducted by Botond Bognar, we can pick out diverse types of creative becomings that nonetheless also frequently interconnect.[1] A "becoming-child" – for example in Takefumi Aida, Kazuhiro Ishii, and Minoru Takeyama – either directly through constructions intended for children or indirectly by drawing inspiration from a childlike vision. A "becoming vegetal," for example in Mayumi Miyawaki, who constructed his *Blue Box* in Tokyo to completely enclose the tops of some large trees, or in Kijo Rokkaku whose *House of Three Roots* has tree trunks and some of their roots emerging, in the raw state, from a cement facade. More generally, we could say that wooden elements are used as symbols of nature by most of the new wave architects. A "becoming-animal" is explicitly asserted by Team Zoo of Waseda University in Tokyo who are influenced by Takmasa Yoshizaka and who,

1. Botond Bognar, *Contemporary Japanese Architecture* (New York: Van Nostrand Reinhold, 1985).

for example, have constructed the *Domo Celakanto* building in the form of a mysterious sea monster. We should also mention a "becoming-abstract" in Tadao Ando, who talks about a "catabolism of landscape," a "becoming-nirvana" in Aida, a politics of light and void in Toyo Ito, a "becoming-nonobject" in Hiromi Fujii and Shinohara, whose conceptualism seeks to bring architecture back to its degree zero, and Mozuna, whose approach is to search for a principle of "anti-dwelling." But concerning all this abundance we only need to refer to Botond Bognar's excellent book. Here I will focus upon the extraordinary "becoming-machine" of Shin Takamatsu, who "devises ingenious and mysterious objects, dangerous reminders that things are not what they seem."[2] Chris Fawcett adds that these objects are all located in cities of western Japan, a fact that is not insignificant given the reserved pride with which the people of the Kyoto region claim their unique talents in the field of aesthetics and, no doubt, in logic as well. Shin Takamatsu is an architect from Kyoto, as he never fails to mention, insisting on the fact that he has been literally shaped by the spirit of this city.[3]

However, there is something that may seem paradoxical in this proclamation since the buildings of Shin Takamatsu are unquestionably among the most provocative that appear in Japan today. Their decorative tubes and steel brooches, parallel bars, metallic adornments, chimneys, glass oculi, their rectangular surfaces that shoot out from the facades like diving boards, the fact, noted by Paul Virilio, that the furniture [*meuble*] merges with the building [*immeuble*].[4] In short, the ensemble of their industrial and futurist aesthetic exhibits no apparent relationship to the city of Kyoto, of which Shin Takamatsu likes to boast about its "impassive softness." A number of critics are put off by such audacities, comparing instead, for example, the extraordinary *ARK* dental clinic (Kyoto, 1983) to a crematorium!

So what kind of relation holds this creator and the urban context in which he works together? Remember that two positions typically confront us when posing this type of question and that

2. S.D., exclusive issue on Shin Takamatsu (Tokyo: Kajima Institute Publishing, 1988), p. 146.
3. S.D., *op. cit.*, p. 57.
4. Introductory blurb on Shin Takamatsu by Paul Virilio on the occasion of his January 1988 exhibition at the Centre Georges Pompidou.

both are subject to endless controversy. There are those who, like Le Corbusier, take the overall context into account such that the arrangement of form establishes the architectural object in a continuous relationship with the urban fabric. And there are those who, like Mies van der Rohe, detach the work from its surrounding environment such that the organization of form depends upon the character of a structuring object.[5]

But perhaps the architecture of the Japanese new wave, and especially that of Shin Takamatsu, leads us to a third possible position in which the work is both complete as an aesthetic object and totally open to its context.[6] This reminds me of the position of a Butoh dancer like Min Tanaka who completely folds in on his body and remains, nevertheless, hypersensitive to every perception emanating from the environment. But, more simply, it is enough to note here that every day we confront such intrinsically structured objects, which don't work with their external environments any less. These objects are none other than the multiple and diverse machines that sustain our entire modern existence. One of their characteristics is that they evolve, substituting one thing for another, over the course of time in a phylogenesis reminiscent of the development of living beings. And with this we remain on the topic of Shin Takamatsu since one of his main imperatives is to reject any idea of style, to never do the same thing twice, to never engage in the same battle with a city without understanding the history that forms a part of its message.[7]

Shin Takamatsu emphasizes the importance of the concept of scale, which he utilizes in a complex way in order to establish systems of correspondence between heterogeneous dimensions, for example, whether elements of the architectural apparatus are in relation to the ensemble of a facade or to the building considered as a whole in relation to the rest of the city.[8] Kyoto, in which light, air, wind, and thought are different and which he apprehends as a fractal organism pulsating on every level in an extraordinarily slow movement, must therefore be secretly rejoined,

5. See Guiseppe Samona's article "Composition architectural" in *Encyclopedia Universalis*, volume II, p. 563.
6. In the sense that Mikhail Bakhtin gives to this expression in his *Esthétique et théorie du roman* (Paris: Gallimard, 1978).
7. S.D., *op. cit.,* p. 61 and statements made in January 1988, *op. cit.*
8. S.D., *op. cit.,* pp. 59 and 61.

recreated, reinvented through each component of its architectural machines.[9] The reference here to Benoit Mandelbrot's fractal objects seems particularly felicitous since, in fact, this type of object effectively implies the existence of internal symmetries or, in other words, forms that can be found at both the macroscopic and microscopic levels.[10] In each element of the architectural ensemble, whether interior or exterior and whatever the size, every ray of light, every possible point of view or angle will therefore contribute to the overall effect.

In fact, in traditional Japanese architecture we find such systems of correspondence between macrocosm and microcosm, interior and exterior. In ancient times, it was inconceivable to construct a religious or official building independently of a garden, or the natural surroundings into which it was placed. For Shin Takamatsu, things are obviously presented otherwise to the extent that, given the circumstances, he must work in a supersaturated urban context. He therefore transfigures the ancient existential relationships between nature and culture by inventing another nature from the urban fabric in response to its hyper-sophisticated creations. One of the most remarkable illustrations of this is the *ARK* dental clinic in Kyoto, which is constructed like a baroque locomotive, simply because of its location adjacent to a railway line and station. It has the effect of transforming the environment, as if by the wave of a magic wand, into a kind of vegetal-machinic landscape.

The work engenders a contextual mutation through its orientation in a direction contrary to common understanding and through its very singularity. Hiromi Fujii, another notable figure of the new wave, has already defined architecture in terms of a machine for producing sense.[11] But it seems to me that, in the case of Shin Takamatsu, we must go further and speak of a machine that produces subjective enunciation or, in other words, existential transferences. Again we find a creative direction firmly rooted in Japanese culture, which consists of passing from one register to another in order to trigger a decentering of the subject. The highest abstraction can therefore be continuous with

9. S.D., *op. cit.*, p. 60.
10. Benoit Mandelbrot, *Les objets fractals* (Paris: Flammarion, 1984).
11. Kenneth Frampton, ed., *The Architecture of Hiromi Fujii* (New York: Rizzoli, 1987).

the most concrete, the most immediate. For example, the stones of the Zen garden at the famous Ryoan-ji temple in Kyoto can be experienced simultaneously as natural elements and as an abstract composition. We could cite numerous other examples of this technology of subjectivity in the traditions of flower arrangement, the tea ceremony, martial arts, Sumo, Noh theater, Bunraku, etc.

Let us now attempt to identify some of the essential components of the processual and resingularizing machines that Shin Takamatsu implements in order to reinvent Japanese subjectivity in its most traditional aspects as well as those concerning an exacerbated modernity.[12] The essential movement made by these immobile machines is that of a break, a separation that opens onto the emergence of new worlds of reference, which in turn engender many existential territories and new collective assemblages of enunciation. In order to attain this existential rupturing and suspension, the most diverse means are employed: ruptures of symmetry, the fitting-together or nesting [*emboîtement*] of decentered forms, horizontal and vertical slits, the separation of the building into two superimposed parts of different styles, steep inclines that drop into a void, abyssal openings, and finally, above all, inserting ocular structures into the facades and interior spaces. The objective remains the same in each case: to arrive at a point where the building becomes a nonhuman subject capable of connecting with segments of individual and collective human subjectivities. Paradoxically, this "becoming-machine" of subjectivity can only be achieved by crossing a threshold, which causes a faciality effect to seize the building, making it live in an animal-animist, vegetal-cosmic manner. Now let's consider each of these machinic components.

Ruptures of symmetry. Broadly speaking, we find in Takamatsu's constructions an almost obsessive repetition of vertical lines (the *Saifukuji* Buddhist temple, Gifu, 1982, or the *ARK* dental clinic, Kyoto, 1983). But these vertical lines are often crossed by diverse transversal elements, for example, by rays of luminous white light in the interior of Dance Hall (Nagoya, 1985) or by

12. Shin Takamatsu likes to affirm his filiation with Italian Futurism and for this purpose he has contrived a curious symbol that we find, in various guises from 1986 forward, in a number of projects he has realized including one called "Killing Moon," a theme inspired by one of Marinetti's poems.

beams suggesting traditional constructions in *Garden* (Kyoto, 1984). On the exterior, we see them on the facade of rectangular columns in *Kitayama Ining 23* (Kyoto 1987) on which are superimposed v-shaped metal beams. In the recent *Migoto* project (planning 1988, construction 1989), this v-form tapers out into a bird's wing and echoes a long flight of stairs seen in profile in the foreground. In the project *Sub-1* (planning 1987, construction 1990), the orthogonal symmetries are systematically derived from quarter circles, half circles, and discontinuous segments.

The fitting-together or nesting of decentered forms. The most frequent combination is that of a cylinder and a cubic structure. The purest and most simple example is the *Kido Clinic* (Kyoto, 1978), where the nesting is perfect. But all variations have been developed: an adjacent cube and cylinder in the *Konmakine House* (Takarazuka, 1977); a cylinder placed perpendicularly beside a rectangular structure in the *Kobolo Lighting Showroom* (Kyoto, 1978); a double facade, where the exterior one is orthogonal and the interior one curved, as in the *Nimura Dyeing Office* (Kyoto, 1979); the superimposition of an enormous cylinder onto a cubic structure (*ARK*, Kyoto, 1983). The nesting is accentuated here due to the extension of the tangent circumference of the facade by a rounded triangular element, which also happens in *M. M. Higashi Gojo S-S* (Kyoto, 1987) except that, in the latter, the cylindrical structure is truncated by a quadrangular form.

Horizontal and vertical slits. This technique, more than just a destabilization of the expected dimensions and forms of ordinary perception, also involves the implementation of a kind of focal attractor for subjectivity. The *Yamamoto Workshop* (Kyoto, 1978), and the *Koboko Lighting Showroom* (Kyoto, 1978), both appear to have been perpendicularly split in two. Dating from the same period, the *Komakine House* (Takarazuka, 1977) has its vertical cylindrical portion split horizontally by an almost continuous window. In 1980 the slit evolves, doubling itself vertically in the *Yamaguchi Photo Studio* (Kyoto) and horizontally in *Pharaoh* (Kyoto, 1984). It is tripled in the *Crystal Palace* project (1988) and even quadrupled in the *Zeus* project (planning 1987, construction 1989), redoubling the two lateral slits.

Separation of the building into two superimposed parts of different styles. This is a more recent method for destabilizing experience by producing a hollowing effect. This is particularly evident in *Yoshida House* (Kyoto, 1982), where a dark ground level tends to merge with the background of an old street, while a massive white superstructure intrudes into the landscape. From 1986, this process is systematically explored. *Origin III* (Kyoto, 1986) even presents a triple superposition of styles. The *Maruto Building* (Tokyo, 1987), as well as at least ten more projects and constructions, continues to build upon this sophisticated stylistic treatment.

Steep inclines that drop into a void. This is a method that we find in other Japanese architects, but what characterizes its use by Shin Takamatsu is its frequently arbitrary character. Whereas the high placement of a traditionally-inspired Japanese lantern poses no problem for the facade of *Takahashi House* (Osaka, 1983), *Pharaoh* (Kyoto, 1984) presents a properly vertiginous interior incline. Sometimes, as in *House at Shugakin II* (Sakyo, Kyoto, 1985), a staircase doubles its image in a mirror and rises majestically only to reach a landing that appears to be an impasse. In the *Syntax* project, the entire building is shaped like an immense staircase leading to two gigantic wings.

Abyssal openings. This is also a frequent treatment of space, of which the oldest and most accentuated dates from 1978 with the *Yamamoto Atelier* (Kyoto, 1978). In 1989, the entire *Yamagushi Photo Studio* (Kyoto) is seemingly devoured by a large cubic buccal assemblage.

Ocular structures. Here the category of windows, openings, and other forms are assigned the role of converting the architectural composition into an enunciative partial object. They complete the facialization of Shin Takamatsu's facades. We find them everywhere: as a cyclopean eye (*Miyahara House*, Kyoto, 1982); as two superimposed eyes (*Pharaoh*, Kyoto, 1984); as two eyes side by side (*Sasaki Confectionary Factory*, Kyoto, 1981); as two machinic eyes of different sizes, offset in relation to each other (*ARK*, Kyoto, 1983); or two eyes merging to form an owl's head as a component of the "'Killing Moon" symbol, which is a kind of signature for Takamatsu (*Origin I*, Kyoto, 1981); as four horizontal eyes, arranged symmetrically in relation to a winged figure, again evoking "Killing Moon" (*Matsui House*, Kyoto, 1986); as four quadrangular eyes shaped by four reflective edges against the background of a curved surface (*Origin II*, Kamigo, Kyoto,

1982); or as a facade entirely covered with eyes that are crossed transversally (*Taketsu cube II, Amagasaki*, 1987). All possible variations are explored, but it should be noted that even in the rare cases where eyes are not explicitly figured, the faciality effect is still sought by other means.

The central question posed by this facialization of buildings is the relation between the psychological and aesthetic aspects of Shin Takamatsu's creations. A compulsive dimension is hinted at in the creative sequencing that arises with each new project. Takamatsu's architectural object is fundamentally decentered in relation to the project plans. It establishes itself beneath rational coherence on the side of a pulsional, virulent core. It is from this unconscious zone that Takamatsu elaborates spatial singularities that are so disconcerting to ordinary perception. The artist himself explains that he is always brought back to the same point of departure – the semiotic mark of ink and paper which will differentiate itself through unexpected bifurcations, erasures, and revisions – in order to gradually acquire the consistency of a process that no longer seems to depend only upon himself. Of course we have yet to explore, in line with the architectural schizzes described above, the constant propensity in Takamatsu's work to go beyond a kind of originary dualism: an obsessive fear of the vertigo of abolition and a fascination with death. But regardless of the importance of the archaic fantasies put into play here, it doesn't seem relevant to insist that they ground, in an essential way, his architectural vision. This is precisely because the object only finds consistency once it has crossed a certain threshold of autonomization and is able to recreate contextual relations in its own terms. This phenomenon is particularly significant in the sumptuous *Kirin Plaza* building (1987), constructed on a site at the edge of a river in Osaka such that both are genuinely transformed by this intrusion. Thus in his pulsional phase, from the initial drawing to the final implementation within the urban fabric, a whole series of mutations in the matter of expression tends to detach the deterritorialized urban object from the psyche that initiated it. In my opinion, it is this detachment and objective self-sufficiency of the architectural machine that constitute the main achievement of Shin Takamatsu's work. (For example, he has frequently restarted finished projects from scratch that had completely satisfied his sponsors simply because some hidden flaw, felt only by the artist, threatened its consistency as an autonomous object). We can therefore distinguish three main phases in the gestation of a work:

- the work of phantasm, which operates primarily through drawing
- the work of delivery as a quasi-exorcism of the architectural object from its phantasmatic roots
- the work of placing its artistic forms in harmony with its external context as well as with its internal and functional purposes

Finally, the most troubling and, it must be acknowledged, sometimes the most perilous aspect – especially of his first major works – lies in the asymmetry of effect between the exterior apprehension and the interior encounter with the same building. We sense that Shin Takamatsu, when struggling with the mystery of the interiority of his constructions, was sometimes caught up in a process that was difficult to master. Occasionally it seems that he might have stopped too soon, which is never the case with his exterior assemblages. But this threat of procrastination is no longer found in the recent works. The breathless pace of these projects takes his fascination with the abyss – in relation to the details of the interior – to the next level (*Orpheus*, Nishio, Aichi, 1987). We might also consider that the future in store for Takamatsu is one of new dialectical *rendez-vous* that will reshuffle, from different angles, this essential problematic of the relationship between interior and exterior.

Singularization and Style:
Shin Takamatsu in Conversation
with Félix Guattari

Félix Guattari: I'd like to discuss the difference between the inside and the outside that I've noticed in many of your projects. How do you deal with the interior-exterior relationship in your process?

Shin Takamatsu: I think that the exterior facade of architecture has a relationship to the outside that includes the street, the environment, and nature. Its meaning is mostly a matter for the public. On the other hand, the interior of architecture can create its own inner system without having a direct relationship to the outside. Therefore a gap forms between the functional role of the exterior to convey messages and the interior. I find the task of designing this gap architecturally very exciting.

Guattari: What do you mean by designing a gap?

Takamatsu: Sometimes the exterior can shatter the perfection of the interior. Something dramatic happens when an exterior light from a space with a foreign morphology enters the interior, instantly preventing the formation of its autonomous world.

Guattari: A world that should be autonomous collapses because there is now a window?

Takamatsu: Yes, that's right. Therefore the word "design" which I used a short while ago may not be appropriate. Actually, I want an element, such as a gap or something dramatic, to reinforce the inner system. I've been trying to get the inside and outside to mutually reinforce each other.

Guattari: However, don't you always begin with the exterior?

Takamatsu: Yes, of course.

Guattari: Do you think that the interior is harder to treat as an object? I mean, do you feel limited by its volume?

Takamatsu: Is volume in fact a spatial aspect?

Guattari: Yes, that's right.

Takamatsu: Most of the interior architectural spaces that I design are spaces subjected to purely centripetal forces. Therefore the various interior scales are reduced while the exterior scales expand until they lose all human scale. If you take a picture of it the outside shrinks towards the centre so the outside looks like a palace that houses a tiny jewel inside.

Guattari: I have the impression that you are now becoming very skillful in the way you design the various elements of the interior compared with your earlier architecture, is that correct? For example, the buildings that I saw yesterday. I think you have designed a larger interior in *Orphe* than in *Origin*.

Takamatsu: It is extremely difficult to construct a contracting space by limiting yourself to the strength of the interior. It's like making myself infinitely smaller. Perhaps because of my age this is getting more and more difficult. Now I have begun to conceptualize a space where the interior space pushes out against the exterior.

Guattari: Because I felt that in *Orphe* the interior and exterior scales were virtually the same.

Takamatsu: That's right. I'm trying to treat the inside as just another outside space in most of the projects upon which I'm currently working. This is a kind of paradox.

Guattari: That's a very important point. I always think that you try to avoid the contrast between outside and inside, and this relates to your process. This brings us to an important idea of creating the context by such a contrast and of trying to escape the system that reduces subjectivity to a product of the interior. I'm extremely interested to know whether you experience a sense of crossing a threshold. I'd like to know, in the concrete stages that lead towards the completion of an architectural structure, whether you surpass the realm of building. Concerning this, do you feel it is more important to design the exterior, the interior, or both equally?

Takamatsu: There is an expectation in architecture that the exterior context should validate the interior structure. I've begun to consider that the narrative and interpretation supported by such a stable scheme are not as rich as I thought. What is important for me now is what exceeds this scheme in order to reach a point where the architecture itself has depth. I find it very difficult to create architecture that does not literally have depth or thickness. My method is to make use of a kind of paradox. I design the exterior to be very dense so that it crosses over into other levels. I'm trying to make thickness and depth by doing this within the field of strength. This is my thrilling and critical struggle with the system of interior and exterior.

Guattari: In my interpretation there are two kinds of processes for creating things, entirely different in character but necessarily intertwined. One process makes you adopt a fantasmatic relation to the object you create. When you commit yourself to fantasy to an excessive degree you lose your sense of scale and the object produced is not architecture. I sense that during the creative process you struggle against the excessive flow of fantasy or that you fight that excess. In the second process, you realize and understand the various operations of correspondence produced between the two scales in an almost paranoid way.

Takamatsu: On which level does this correspondence take place?

Guattari: On every level, from the whole to the structure's various elements. You seem to me to confront excess by not suppressing either of these two dialectical stages. I'd like to know how you process the difference between drawing something on paper and your pure imagination? An imagination that creates forms like a human face or an animal's body for example. I mean, how do you make your imagination and the various practical demands coexist when you draw despite the split that exists between them?

Takamatsu: In the case of my design work it is not possible to distinguish between these two things. I suppose there is something like an abstract idea of architecture. I think it is possible to make all these things resonate together by using the various systems of architecture itself, to issue a challenge to everything that accomplishes architectural space, including the exterior and interior relationship. In these attempts, imagination, which comes close to delusion, becomes a tool, or sometimes the intentional misuse of what is known or the misuse of scale becomes a certain tool. There are various levels of tools useful for disturbing the abstract idea of architecture, from the conscious to the unconscious.

Guattari: This is very interesting. I'd like to ask you one more question. Do you agree that ultimately you live in the object as if it was your very existence?

Takamatsu: What do you mean?

Guattari: For example, your staff told me that you often redesign a project again and again, despite it having already satisfied the client. In short, was it that you couldn't make yourself live in the object?

Takamatsu: In that sense, yes, I think so.

Guattari: This is actually related to a very important theme for me. I think it is possible that writing and drawing are the same thing. In the system of signs, denotation and signification distinguish two functions. Denotation is the relation that uses indication to describe the object directly. But signification doesn't point directly to the intentional object, there is a discontinuity between the signification and the intentional object.

Takamatsu: I have expressed this gap with the phrase "diversional event" because I think architecture is a kind of sign system.

Guattari: For linguists the signified and the signifier have an arbitrary relationship. There is no existential relation between pencil as a phoneme and the pencil itself. Or rather, a system of correspondence doesn't exist, or if it exists, it would only be a system of arbitrary connections. This contradicts the conventional point of view. I want to propose that we should try to grasp another dimension, another level. I call denotation the first category, signification the second, and I've added a third which I call the existential function. For example, this function establishes an autonomous subjectivity for architecture such as *Kirin Plaza*. The subjectivation creates an existential domain in the same way that it creates yourself. Therefore you would be living in your architecture. And this autonomous function must undoubtedly also work for people who live there or who pass by.

Takamatsu: I think that this distance is probably an equidistance that has always existed between architecture, the architect, and those who live there or pass by. This separation makes it possible to activate the autonomous function.

Guattari: Yes, for example I think it is the same for subjectivity in music. I think the same distance exists between a piece of music, those who play it, and those who listen to it. In short, there is an automatic system of self-reference at work. In general, the object can't escape from the system of external reference, however, the existential system can escape it completely. This existential object is continuously exposed to the threat of death or annihilation because the object which has the function of self-reference is different from the normal object in that it can exist on the border of heterogeneous spaces making it possible for it to vanish. Your architecture is like this; in other words, separation at the semantic level has occurred somewhere. For me it is a very interesting point that a semantic separation from the system of signs has occurred. The function of denotation and signification no longer works and the separation between the two itself begins to move, i.e., the system of reference is like this, various structures join together and only start functioning by combining their mutual strengths and this gives rise to subjectivity. In my opinion your subjectivity has the structure of this kind of reference system. The problem is finding a standard for making decisions and having control. The solution is none other than the individual fantasy or archaism, in other words a psychological standard for control. It is a matching of scales on two levels, on one hand the level of individual creation and on the other the level of various architectural factors. These standard functions join with the functions of an existential domain and because of that a correspondence is born between the individual level and the level that people sense when inhabiting that space.

Takamatsu: Yes, I think that's right.

Guattari: I think it is very important that people work in the direction I have just explained, otherwise everything will end up in a psychological dimension. The psychological dimension is however only one of the constituents of the creative process. I think you must have your own internal logic, could you tell me about that?

Takamatsu: There are several dimensions that can be considered regarding my methodology. There is the dimension of archaic fantasy, various mathematical dimensions, references which support the architectural sign system, as well as other dimensions. It is impossible to mediate between all these dimensions. Even when designing a single small dwelling I have to traverse between the mixture of those layers of dimensions. This word "traverse" has the same meaning as resonance used earlier. However, even when the resonance has a large amplitude there is almost always an instance when it does not work. This can be expressed in the following way, the various dimensions have become electrified and reach a critical point where they face collapse. I believe at that point subjectivity establishes itself. That may be why my architecture produces a dense nothingness.

Guattari: Japanese philosophy has the concept of *mu* (nothing, empty) as well as *kyoko* (figment, falseness). There are many people who emphasize the metaphysics of nothingness or emptiness in contemporary Japanese architecture. Your dense nothingness is different from that kind of nothingness.

Takamatsu: Yes, that's right.

Guattari: One other thing, in addition to those levels there is the burden of your past. You said just now that you traverse various levels such as economic, social, and mathematical systems, but in addition to those levels your career as an architect up until now has accumulated a past despite your attitude of always trying to change, these temporal factors would also form a level that has to be traversed. I've heard that you say you don't have your own style. I don't think that is such an easy thing to say. I mean, regardless of you denying that you have a style, the result will be that you gradually accumulate a style.

Takamatsu: I have begun to feel strongly that there is a kind of stream beginning to form inside of me, because of this my methods are changing somewhat. Perhaps you could say that I've lost track of the speed of the stream, in other words, I'm going with the flow of the stream, moving at the same speed as the stream rather than faster or going a little bit upstream.

Guattari: Looking at your recent architecture I get this feeling, for example, with the pillars of Saifukuji, however continuing our discussion about your style, even if style is a personal burden for you, your style is playing a role in contemporary Japanese architecture. In other words, the impression I get is that you first appeared as a somewhat unusual outsider and this position changed as you completed more and more projects. Because you are carrying the burden of Japanese contemporary architecture on your shoulders and pushing it to the limit you are no longer an outsider of architecture. Rather, I think you are standing in a position where you can speak as a representative of contemporary architecture. I think that the burden of style has that meaning.

Takamatsu: I would like to pay careful attention to those circumstances. It is always necessary to step out from my internal stream and also from the external stream which is quite different. Before I talked about repeating my steps and making a little progress, by paying attention to that you can start to make a slight difference in the flow of the stream. These slight differences give rise to a strong desire to stand outside, to move from one subjectivity to another.

Guattari: It's a kind of resonance, isn't it? In the final analysis most people who have seen your architecture are surprised by the shape of strange machines or say that it is a strange fantastic piece of architecture, which is definitely its major characteristic, but it is not enough to look only at the level of psychological constituents. It is necessary to re-examine your architecture as a process of singularization. By doing that your architecture will then be the effect of a singularization that creates a characteristic fantasy that will capture everyone, all architects, and be shared by many kinds of people. At this point I think it would be interesting if you created your own school. Perhaps the same kind of system will be triggered in the people who gather around you and each one of those people will encounter their own singularization.

Takamatsu: Isn't this singularization the construction of an overwhelming distance by internalizing an object, in this case the autonomous system of architecture?

Guattari: I think that this distance is the same as what I was calling scale. Generally speaking, in the objective world the various distances are the differences between something and something else outside of it, therefore we have to separate ourselves from spatial or temporal forces, in other words the relation to the outside, and focus directly on the forces using our internal forces. Let me take another example from music. Performers study the score in detail, they consider their own performance technique, they consider their relationship to the orchestra and the desires of the audience, and finally they consider their own emotions. These various different dimensions resonate together at a point in time producing a harmony which gives us the autonomy of a musical object. At that time the composition begins to function by itself without regard for the outside. This, in a manner of speaking, is a recognition due to a transference, it is a recognition based on concepts. You can also say that it is an understanding based on emotions and not on concepts. Having said that, it is not a vague emotion but an extremely accurate and appropriate emotion. It is appropriate because it corresponds to our understanding which is firmly tied to the existential domain made up of various different worlds. Projecting into the future, it will be very interesting to see how your very individualistic architecture will change when you start to work on hospitals, mental health clinics, schools, etc. In other words, I would like to see how the various factors in those systems would enter into your design process.

Takamatsu: Can architecture give itself up to the architect? I have asked my wife, who is a doctor, how to go about answering that question. Her advice was short and clear. She advised in the case of a hospital to put yourself in the place of a patient. Listening to your talk today I began to think about what she said. Can you imagine a conversation between an architect who designs functional buildings like hospitals and one who designs buildings very different from that kind of functional building?

Guattari: No I can't, I'm not an architect. However, to a certain extent the answer to that question can be found in what we were talking about before. So-called functionalist modern architecture gave priority to function, and singularization at the architectural level was given a lower priority. In your case, singularization at the architectural level takes precedence. So I think the answer will follow from that. For example the mental clinic where I work is a very old building that was not designed to be a hospital, so from the functional point of view it leaves a lot to be desired. That is because buildings are intended for the purposes for which they were built. However, on the other hand, rooms and hallways can take on various new and singular functions. Spaces lose their original human characteristics and can be recreated by the people who are there now. In this sense it can be said that in the period when the building was not a hospital the building had less possibility for singularization and autonomization. Can you imagine a future architecture and a virtual architecture?

Takamatsu: When teaching architecture to university students I always come up against a great barrier, even though there are instances when communication is instantaneous, but this is definitely not because of any universal understanding. It is a very particular discovery or communication. It could also be said that this was the construction of a virtual architecture within architecture itself.

Guattari: I think that is because singularity invites new singularities, contrary to universality that presupposes consensus.

Ecosophical Practices and the Restoration of the "Subjective City"

Contemporary human beings have been fundamentally deterritorialized. Their original existential territories – bodies, domestic spaces, clans, cults – are no longer secured by a fixed ground; but henceforth they are indexed to a world of precarious representations and in perpetual motion. Young people are walking around the streets with *Walkmans* glued to their ears, and are habituated by refrains produced far, very far, from their homelands. Their homeland – anyway, what could that mean to them? It is surely not the place where their ancestors have lived since time immemorial; neither is it the place where they were born, nor where they will die. They no longer have ancestors: they have disappeared without knowing why, just as they themselves will vanish. An informatic code has been allocated that will program a predetermined socio-professional trajectory for them, and some will be relatively privileged and others less so.

Everything circulates: music, fashion, advertising slogans, gadgets, "bits" of information, industrial subsidiaries; and at the same time, everything seems to remain in place, staying where it is, so the differences become indistinct between places of manufacturing and within standardized spaces where everything is interchangeable. Tourists, for example, travel mostly without moving, using the same *pullmans*, airplane cabins, air-conditioned hotel rooms, and simply pass before the monuments and landscapes that they have encountered a hundred times before on their television screens or in some travel brochure. Subjectivity finds itself threatened by paralysis. It loses the taste for difference, the unpredictable, and for the singular event. TV game shows, the *star system* in sport, variety shows, political life, work on subjectivity like neuroleptic drugs which guard against anxiety at the price of infantilization and de-responsibilization.

Will human beings regret the loss of the stable landmarks of not long ago? Must we hope for the sudden blow of the end of history; must we accept as fate the return to nationalism, conservatism, and to xenophobia, that is, of racism and fundamentalism? While notable fractions of popular opinion are today struck by such temptations, this does not render them less illusory and dangerous. In this situation, new transcultural, transnational, and transversal earths and universes of value may be formed, unencumbered by the fascination of territorialized power, that can be separated from the outcomes of the current planetary impasse. Humanity and the biosphere go hand-in-hand together, and the future of one and the other are equally tributaries of the mechanosphere which envelops them. That is to say, one cannot hope to recompose a humanly inhabitable earth without the reinvention of economic and productive finalities, urban assemblages, social, cultural, artistic and mental practices. The infernal machine of a blind, quantitative economic belief, free of any concern for its human and ecological consequences, and placed under the exclusive aegis of a profit-driven economy and neoliberalism, must give way to a new type of qualitative development, rehabilitating the singularity and the complexity of the objects of human desire. I have baptized one such concatenation of environmental, scientific, economic, urban and social and mental ecologies: ecosophy. Not in order to incorporate all of these heterogeneous ecological approaches in the same totalizing or totalitarian ideology, but, to indicate, on the contrary, the prospect of an ethico-political choice of diversity, creative dissensus, of responsibility concerning difference and alterity. Each segment of life, while continuing to be inserted into the transindividual phylums which exceed it, is fundamentally understood in its uniqueness. Birth, death, desire, love, the relationship to time, to bodies, to both animate and inanimate forms, demand a fresh look, unsullied, and receptive. It is incumbent upon us to reproduce continuously this subjectivity that the psychoanalyst and ethologist of childhood, Daniel Stern, calls the "emergent self."[1] Recapturing childhood glances and poetry instead, and in the place of, the hard and blind perspective on the meaning of life according to the expert and technocrat. Here it is not a question of opposing the utopia of a new "Celestial Jerusalem," like that of the Apocalypse, to the harsh realities of our era, but of establishing a "subjective City" at the very heart of these realities, by reorienting technological, scientific, economic, and international ends (in particular the relations between North and South) and the great mass mediatic machines. We shake free from a false nomadism that in reality leaves us back where we started from, in the emptiness of a bloodless modernity, in order to access lines of flight of desire where machinic, communicational, and aesthetic deterritorializations, engage us. In this way, creating the conditions of emergence, on the occasion of a reappropriation of the forces of our world, of an existential nomadism as intense as that of the Pre-Columbian American Indians or Australian Aboriginals!

This collective reorientation of human activities depends in large part on the evolution of urban mentalities. The futurists are predicting, in effect, that within the next decade, nearly 80% of the population worldwide will live in urban agglomerations. From this point of view, it is reasonable to add that the remaining 20% of the "rural" population will nevertheless remain dependent upon the economy and technologies of cities. In fact, the distinction between city/nature will be profoundly modified, "natural" territories subsisting dependently to a large extent on "programming": tourism, leisure activities, sports, cottages, eco-preserves, and telematically diffused industrial activities. Nature must be cared for permanently on the same level as urban environments. In a general way, serious threats to the biosphere (geoclimatic modifications, increase of carbon dioxide in the atmosphere and destruction of the ozone layer), worldwide demographic pressures, and the international division of labor will change the way that urbanites think through their particular problems in terms of planetary ecology. Is this hegemonic power of cities

---

1. Daniel Stern, *The Interpersonal World of the Infant* (New York: Basic Books, 1985).

necessarily synonymous with homogenization, amalgamation, and sterile subjectivity? In the future, how do we reconcile ourselves with the energies of singularization and reterritorialization which today find only a pathological expression in a growing nationalism, tribalism and religious fundamentalism?

Let us recognize, too, that this tendency of cities toward hegemonic power is not a recent development! Since ancient times, the great cities exercised their powers against developing countries, barbarian nations and nomadic ethnic groups (for example, the Roman Empire, within and beyond its "*limes*" [borders]). However, during these epochs, the distinctions between urban and non-urban civilization remained generally well marked, setting off religious and political struggles. In his book, *Living Space in Japan*, Augustin Berque delicately illustrates the tendencies of the traditional urban Japanese society to withdraw both from "the deep forest and its chimera" and from every adventure beyond the sea.[2] But times have changed. Numerous Japanese mountain climbers scale the summits of the Himalayas and the Japanese economic and cultural sectors reach into the four corners of the globe.

Throughout history, one cannot speak of a rapport – in the sense that they spoke with one voice – between cities and rural areas. Cities interfered in every area of civilization. Thus, in the 16th Century, there was a veritable proliferation of city models correlative to the emergence of processes of urbanization and the collective apparatuses of the great national capitalistic entities. This diversification of cities barely touches on the typologies developed by the historian Fernand Braudel; nevertheless, on the condition that utilizing a combination of them is to put into play heterogeneous factors – apart from questions of size and rank – brings us back to the functions of collective apparatuses which we should consider here. Let us look, for example, following Braudel, at the diversity of Spanish cities he studied in his book *The Mediterraneans and the Mediterranean World*.[3]

Granada and Madrid were bureaucratic cities; Toledo, Burgos and Seville were equally bureaucratic but, in addition, full of people with private incomes and with craftspersons. Bordou and

2. Augustin Berque, *Vivre l'espace au Japon* (Paris: P.U.F., 1982).
3. Fernand Braudel, *La méditerranée et le monde méditerranéen* (Paris: Armande Colin, 1966).

100

Segovia were industrialized and capitalistic; Cuenca was industrial with cottage industries, whereas Salamanca and Jerez were agricultural cities, and Guadalajura was a clerical city. Further, other cities were oriented toward the military, "sheep farming," rustic pursuits, seasides, and scholarly study.... Finally, the only way to make all these diverse cities hold together in the same capitalistic ensemble is to consider them as several components of the same national network of collective apparatuses.

Nowadays, the material and immaterial apparatuses of networks are woven together at a scale much greater than a national network. And, the more such a network is globalized and digitalized, the more it is standardized and rendered uniform. Braudel describes a sort of historical migration of "world-cities" that successively exercise an economic and cultural domination over the world economy: Venice in the middle of the 14th century; Anvers in the middle of the 16th century; Amsterdam at the beginning of the 18th century, and London since the end of the 18th century.... According to Braudel, capitalistic markets were deployed in concentric zones starting from urban centers which held the economic keys, allowing them to capture most of the surplus value; whereas they tended toward a sort of degree zero closer to their peripheral areas, as prices reached a maximum due to lethargic exchanges. This situation concerning the concentration of capitalistic power in a single world-city was profoundly modified in the last third of the 20th century. In the future, in fact, there will no longer be a localized center dominating the worldwide economy, but a hegemony of an "archipelago of cities" or, to be more precise, sub-ensembles of large cities connected by telematic and informatic means. The world-city of the new figure of integrated worldwide capitalism is deeply deterritorialized, and its diverse components are scattered over every surface of a multipolar urban rhizome encircling the planet.

The networking of capitalistic power worldwide, in homogenizing its urban and communicational apparatuses and the mentalities of its elites, has also exacerbated differences of status among neighborhoods. Inequalities no longer necessarily change from a center to its periphery, but between technologically and informatically over-equipped urban enclaves and areas of middle-class mediocrity, and sometimes those of catastrophical impoverishment. In Rio, mere tens of meters separate rich neighborhoods and favelas. In New York, the head offices of international financial firms at the top of Manhattan coexist with real zones of underdevelopment in Harlem and the South Bronx where streets and public parks are invaded by tens of thousands of "homeless." It was still common in the 19th century for the poor to live on the top levels of residences while the other floors were occupied by wealthy families. Whereas, today, social segregation works in terms of an enclosure in ghettos, as in Sanya in the heart of Tokyo, or in the Kamagasaki quarter in Osaka, or in the poorest suburbs of Paris. Certain Third World countries are even becoming like concentration camps, or, at the very least, zones of house arrest for populations that are not permitted to leave their countries. But it needs to be added that, capitalistic representations even find the means to penetrate the immense shantytowns of the Third World through the biases of television, gadgets, and drugs. The positions of master and slave, poor and rich, affluent and underdeveloped, tend to jointly develop in visible urban space, in formations of power, and in alienated subjectivities. The capitalistic deterritorialization of the city therefore represents only an intermediate stage; it establishes itself on the basis of a rich/poor reterritorialization. It is not a matter of dreaming of a return to the walled medieval cities, but to move, on the contrary, in the direction of a supplementary deterritorialization, shifting the city toward new universes of value, to confer on it as a fundamental goal a production of a non-segregative and resingularized subjectivity, that is to say, ultimately, liberated from the hegemony of a capitalistic valorization solely based on profit. This is not to say that all of the regulations of the market must necessarily be abandoned.

One must admit that the persistence of misery is not a simple residual fact, more or less passively endured by affluent societies. Poverty is required by the capitalist system which uses it as a device for setting the collective force of labor in motion. The individual is expected to submit to urban disciplines, to the demands of wage-earning or to income from capital. He is expected to occupy a certain rank on the social scale, otherwise he will sink into the depths of poverty, dependency and, eventually, delinquency. Collective subjectivity controlled by capitalism is thus polarized in a field of value: rich/poor; autonomous/dependent; integration/disintegration. But is this system of hegemonic valorization the only conceivable one? Is it the indispensable corollary to the entire consistency of the socius? Can we not envisage the emancipation of other modes of valorization (solidarity value, aesthetic value, ecological value …)? It is precisely toward a redeployment of values that ecosophy will work. Motivations other than the atrocious menace of poverty must be able to promote the division of labor and the engagement of individuals in socially acknowledged activities. Such an ecosophical refoundation of practices will rise in tiers from the most everyday, personal, familial and neighborhood levels up to geopolitical stakes and planetary ecologies. It will call into question the separation of the civilian and the military, the ethical and the political. It will require the redefinition of collective assemblages of enunciation, through dialogue and execution. It will not only "change life," according to the countercultural dream of the 1960s, but also change the way of doing urbanism, education and psychiatry, and the way of doing politics and conducting international relations. We will therefore not have recourse to "spontaneist" conceptions or to simplistic self-management. The issue is that of holding together a complex organization consisting of society and the mode of production, with a mental ecology and interpersonal relations of a new type.

The future of planetary urbanization seems to be marked by features that will often evolve in contradictory directions:

- **An intensification of gigantism** synonymous with an overextension and fouling of internal and external communications and an increase in pollution which already reaches intolerable levels;
- **A "contraction" of communicational space** (Paul Virilio calls it the "dromosphere")[4] on account of the acceleration of the speed of transportation and the intensification of the means of telecommunication;
- **An exacerbation of global inequalities** between the urban areas of rich countries and those of the Third World, and an even more marked accentuation of these

---

4. Paul Virilio, *Vitesse et politique* (Paris: Galilée, 1977).

disparities around the same cities between wealthy areas and poor ones, that will create more serious problems associated with crime and the maintenance of security for people and property; the constitution of relatively uncontrolled urban areas on the edges of large cities;

A double movement:

- involving populations within national borders, accompanied by stronger control measures at the borders and airports, illegal immigration, and limitations on immigration, expulsion of immigrants without proper visas or passports;
- a tendency running contrary to urban nomadism;
- daily nomadism (commuting) between home and work, which has the effect in Tokyo at least of furthering land speculation;
- nomadism of labor, for example between Alsace and Germany, or between Los Angeles, San Diego, and Mexico;
- nomadic pressure of populations from the Third World and countries of the Eastern bloc moving to developed countries.

In the future, the movements qualified as nomadic will be more and more difficult to control and thus a source of ethnic friction, racism and xenophobia.

- **Constitution of "tribalized" urban subgroups**, or more precisely, those centered on one or more categories of populations of foreign origin. For example, in the US, Chinatowns, Puerto Rican barrios, Black ghettos, etc.

The growth of certain cities, like Mexico City, that in a few more years will reach a population of 30 million inhabitants, and has record levels of pollution and congestion, seems to be up against insurmountable obstacles. Other wealthy cities, like those in Japan, envisage bringing enormous resources to bear upon the remodeling of their layouts. But responses to these problems outstrip the scope of both urbanism and economics, and require the mobilization of socio-politics, ecology, and ethics.

104

Cities have become giant machines, "megamachines," to borrow an expression from Lewis Mumford,[5] producers of individual and collective processes of subjectivation by means of collective apparatuses (education, health, social control, culture …) and mass media. The material infrastructure, communications and services of cities cannot be separated from functions that may be described as existential. Megamachines model sensibility, intelligence, inter-relational style, and even unconscious phantasms. Hence, the importance of bringing about a transdisciplinary collaboration between urbanists, architects, and all the other disciplines of the social, human, and ecological sciences. The urban drama being played out on the horizon at the end of the millennium is only one aspect of a crisis much more fundamental that threatens the future of humankind around the planet. Without a radical reorientation of methods, and particularly goals of production, the global biosphere will be thrown out of balance and develop toward a state of total incompatibility with human life and all forms of animal and vegetable life in general. This reorientation urgently suggests an unbending stance on, in particular, both the chemical and energy industries; a limitation on automobile traffic or the invention of a means of pollution-free transportation; and the cessation of large-scale deforestation. In truth, it is the spirit of economic competition between individuals, companies, and nations that is to blame.

Present day ecological consciousness still influences only a minority of opinion, although the mass media is beginning to recognize it, and the stakes are being progressively clarified. However, we are still far from a strategic global willingness that would be operationally capable of taking up and bringing into its wake the leading political and economic powers. There is, rather, a kind of sprinting between human collective consciousness, the instinct for the survival of humanity, and a catastrophe that could bring about the end of human life on earth before the end of a few decades! This outlook makes our epoch at once disquieting but also passionate, since ethico-political factors throw into relief issues that we have never had to confront throughout history.

I do not know how best to underscore the fact that ecological consciousness ought not to be satisfied with worrying about

5. Lewis Mumford, *La cité à travers l'histoire,* trans. Guy Durand and Gérard Durand (Paris: Seuil, 1961).

environmental factors, such as atmospheric pollution, the predictable consequences of global warming, and the extinction of animals; it also ought to bear upon ecological devastation in the social and mental domains. Without transforming mentalities and collective habits, there will only be "remedial" measures taken concerning the material environment.[6]

Southern countries are the principal victims of these ecological devastations, because of the absurd system which currently presides over international exchanges. For example, control of the catastrophic demographic pressure that the majority of them think is tied, for the most part, to their release from economic paralysis, and to the promotion of harmonious development as a substitute for the goal of blind growth, and profit. Ultimately, wealthy countries have nothing to gain from such politics, but how will they become aware of the abyss into which their leaders plunge them? Fear of the catastrophe, bugbear of the end of the world, is not necessarily the best counsel in such matters. The investment fifty years ago by the Japanese, Italian and German masses in the suicidal ideology of fascism, has shown us too well

---

6. Guattari's parenthetical remarks: "In Japan, you are perhaps less sensitive to this aspect of things to the extent that your technological revolution is accompanied by a certain conservatism including ways of being and thinking. However, it is also true that there exist here as elsewhere a considerable number of psychological and sociological problems concerning, in particular:

- Women's issues;
- Minorities on the margins of society (like Burakumin and the Ainu people);
- Conditions of children in the school system;
- Conditions of seniors.

Anyway, you must realize that wherever these kinds of problems exist, their seriousness only tends to deepen. At this juncture, the feelings of loneliness, abandonment, and existential emptiness perfusing the countries of Europe and states of the US must be addressed. The lives of millions of unemployed workers and people requiring social assistance are rendered hopeless, surrounded by a society for which the only finality is the production of goods or standardized cultural assets, none of which allow the blossoming and development of human potentialities. Once again, I repeat that people cannot rebuild healthy relationships with the biosphere unless they are also willing to rebuild society and the psyche."

that the catastrophe is truly catastrophic, a sort of vertigo of collective death.

Therefore, it is paramount that a new progressive axis, crystallizing around the positive values of ecosophy, prioritizes finding a solution to the moral poverty and to the loss of meaning that inevitably infects displaced, non-guaranteed populations, in the very midst of the citadels of capitalism. It is necessary to describe the feeling of solitude, of neglect, and existential emptiness that perfuses both Europe and the US. Millions of unemployed, and welfare recipients, live desperate lives in the midst of societies whose only prerogatives are the production of material goods and standardized cultural objects, which do not contribute to the blossoming of human potentialities.

Today, urbanists can no longer be satisfied with defining cities in spatial terms. The urban phenomenon has changed nature. It is no longer one problem among many. It is problem number one: the problem sitting at the crossroads of economic, social, cultural, and ideological stakes. The city forges the destiny of humanity through its social advancements and segregations, the formation of its elites, the future of social innovation, and of creation in all fields. Quite frequently, we fail to appreciate this global aspect of its problematics. Politicians tend to assign these questions to specialists. A certain tendentious evolution is the result. In France, under the pressure of ecologists, on both the right and the left, a kind of recentering of political life can be seen on the local level. The debates in parliament tend to pass to the second level, compared with existing stakes in the large cities and the areas around them. There also exists, in a latent state, a sort of aristocracy of deputy-mayors of French cities set against the major political powers concentrated in the capital. But it is not yet acting officially there; it is only a timid evolution that could ultimately overthrow a lot of the deeper levels of political life as a whole.

One of the principal driving forces of future urban transformation will also be found in the invention of new technologies, above all in the intersections between the audiovisual, informatic and telematic. Briefly, in the near future, we may see:

1) the possibility of carrying out from home the greatest variety of duties with different off-site partners via tele-connectivity;

2) the development of "visiophony" in correlation with the synthesis of the human voice, which will simplify the use of tele-services, allowing access to data banks, which will relay libraries, archives, and information services;

3) the generalization of tele-distribution by cable or telephone giving access to a large number of programs in the fields of leisure, education, training, and information, as well as home shopping;

4) the means for making immediate contact with travelers wherever they are in the world;

5) new methods of transportation will appear that are non-polluting and combine public systems with the advantages of individual transportation devices (integrated convoys of individual vehicles, high speed conveyor belts, small programmed vehicles circulating within particular sites);

6) the clear separation between levels and sites intended for transportation and those for pedestrian use;

7) new methods of transportation for merchandise (pneumatic tubes and conveyor belts permitting, for example, home delivery of goods).[7]

Regarding new materials, construction in the future will allow more and more audacious designs to be realized, and a great architectural and urbanistic audacity will be irrevocably linked with the struggle to eliminate industrial pollution and hazardous substances (engaging water treatment, scales of biodegradability, removal of toxins from food and household cleaning supplies, etc.)

Consider some of the factors that put the accent on the city as a means of the production of subjectivity through new ecosophical practices:

1) **Revolutions in informatics, robotics, telematics, and biotechnology** will drive the exponential growth of every form of production of material and immaterial goods. But this production will occur without the creation of a new volume of employment, as Jacques Robin's book, *Change Era*,[8] clearly proved. In

---

7. Joël de Rosnay, *Les rendez-vous du futur* (Paris: Fayard, 1991).

8. Jacques Robin, *Changer d'ère* (Paris: Seuil, 1989). See the discussion between Guattari and Robin, "Révolution informationnelle, écologie et recomposition subjective," *Multitudes* 24 (Printemps 2006). http://multitudes.samizdat.net/Revolution-informationnelle. [TN]

these conditions, greater amounts of time will become available and devoted to unstructured activities. But for what exactly? An insignificant "little bit of work," as French authorities have imagined it? Otherwise, in order to develop new social relationships of solidarity such as mutual aid, neighborly relations, new activities for protecting the environment, a new conception of culture, less passivity in front of television, more active, more creative....

2) **This first factor will be reinforced** by the consequences of the very strong demographical push that will be maintained, on a planetary scale, over several decades essentially in the impoverished countries, that will then exacerbate the contradiction between the countries where "something happens" economically and culturally, and the desolate "have-not" countries and passive recipients of aid. In the latter, the question of the reconstruction of forms of sociality destroyed by capitalism, colonialism and imperialism, will be sharply posed. An eminent role will be devolved, in this respect, to renewed forms of cooperation.

3) **In the opposite direction, we will witness a pronounced demographic collapse** in the developed countries (North America, Europe, Australia …). In France, for example, the fertility rate has declined about 30% since 1950. This demographical drop is parallel to a veritable decomposition of traditional family structures (a decrease in the number of marriages, increase of cohabitation without marriage, increase in the divorce rate, progressive disappearance of family relationships as children have families and move far away from their parents). This isolation of individuals and nuclear families has never been compensated by the creation of new social relations. Informal social relations among neighbors, life within associations, trade unions, and religious groups remains stagnant and are generally decreasing, yet compensated, if I may say so, by a passive and infantile consumption of mass media. What remains of the family has become an often regressive and conflictual refuge. The new individualism imposed in developed societies, inside the family circle, is not synonymous with social liberation. In this register, architects, sociologists and psychologists will need to reflect on what might become a resocialization of individuals, a reinvention of the social framework, with the proviso that, and in all likelihood, there should not be a return to the recomposition of

older family structures and outdated corporative relationships, etc.[9]

4) **Burgeoning information technologies and remote order and delivery controls** will allow envisioning the hierarchical relationships currently existing between cities and between quarters of the same city in a different way. For example, at present, more than 80% of large and medium enterprises with branches located on every point of French territory are concentrated in Paris, whereas, the second largest city in France, Lyon, has less than 3% of the decision-making power, and no other city attains even 2%. Telematic transmissions could modify this abusive centralization. At the same time, one can see that in every relevant area of democratic life, and on every scale, including the most local, some new forms of telematic exchanges are emerging.

5) **In the fields of culture and education**, access to a multitude of cable channels, data banks, films, etc. could open up great possibilities, especially when it comes to institutional creativity.

But each of these new perspectives would make sense only on the condition that true social experimentation takes the lead role, conducting an evaluation and a collective reappropriation, enriching individual and collective subjectivity, rather than work, as is unfortunately quite often the case, with current mass media, in the sense of a reductionism, standardization, and a general impoverishment of the "subjective City."[10]

---

9. Louis Roussel, "L'avenir de la famille," *La recherche* 14 (October 1989), pp. 1248-1253.

10. Guattari's parenthetical remark: "Interesting experiments like "Perestroika" are actually under way in the USSR, in the context of a situation which for a long time was blocked by bureaucracy and the limits of politicians. These experiments are coordinated by a Center of Regional Research created by the Science Academy under the leadership of Victor Tischenko. The activities of these groups brought about the cooperatives that constructed, in Moscow, Leningrad and other cities, apartments with better conditions than those built by the State. In 1987, at the demand of the deputy, Boris Yeltsin, they took a big gamble to make the City of Moscow become more social, and 150 persons participated from every level of the social hierarchy to define a new methodology on the question of city planning. The purpose of such "role playing" was to make everyone understand that power can become the articulation of multiple partners proceeding by alliance and negotiation rather than relations of domination between the branches of a hierarchical system from which none can escape."

I suggest that, when programs for new cities are set out and old areas are renovated or disused industrial buildings are converted, important contracts of research and social experimentation should be established not only with social scientists, but also with a certain number of future residents and users of these buildings, in order to study the possibilities for new styles of domestic life, new practices for neighbors, education, culture, sports, child care, geriatric care, patients, etc.

In fact, the means to change life and create a new style of activity, with new social values, are very close at hand. The only deficiency is the desire and political willingness to realize such transformations. These new practices concern the time freed up by modern machinism, new conceptions about relationships with children, the condition of women, the elderly, and cross-cultural relationships…. The precondition to such changes resides in the awareness that it is possible and necessary to alter the current state of affairs and there is nothing more urgent. It is only in a climate of openness and emulation that experiments on new ways of dwelling can take place, and not by force of law and technocratic circulars. Correlatively, such a remodeling of urban life implies that profound transformations should take place in the planetary division of labor and that, in particular, a number of Third World countries should no longer be treated as international aid ghettos. It is equally necessary that outdated international antagonisms are wound down, resulting in a general political disarmament that will permit the transfer of considerable funds for experimentation toward a new urbanism.

A point I would like to particularly insist upon is the emancipation of women. The reinvention of a social democracy is, for the most part, based on the fact that women should be in a position to assume responsibility at every level of society.[11] The exacerbation, by education and the media, of the psychological and social disparities between men and women, which place men in the value system of competition and women, on the contrary, in a passive position, is a synonym for a certain misrecognition of the relation to space as the locus of existential well-being. A new gentleness, a new attentiveness to the other in its difference and singularity, is still to be invented.

11. Guattari's parenthetical remark: "I salute the awakening of Japanese opinion on this question."

Do we have to wait for global political transformations before undertaking molecular revolutions that will converge on changing mentalities? We find ourselves in a doubly difficult situation: on one hand, society, politics, and the economy cannot be changed without a mutation of mentalities; but, on the other hand, mentalities can only be truly changed if global society follows a movement of transformation. The social experimentation on the grand scale that we are advocating will constitute one of the means of escaping from this contradiction. A few successful experiments in new living conditions will have considerable consequences for stimulating a general willingness to change. (This has been the case, for example, in the field of education, with the "initiatic" experiment of Celestin Freinet, who has totally reinvented the space of school classrooms.) Essentially, the urban object is very complex and demands that we face it with methodologies appropriate to such complexity. Social experimentation aims at particular species of "strange attractors" comparable to those of the physics of chaotic processes.[12] A "mutant" objective order can emerge from the actual chaos of our cities, but so can a new poetry, a new art of living. This "logic of chaos" requires fully taking into account situations in their singularity. It is a matter of entering into processes of re-singularization and of the irreversibilization of time.[13] In addition, it is a question of building, not only in the real but also in the possible, according to the bifurcations that can prepare the way; building, that is, by giving chances to virtual mutations to lead future generations to live, feel and think in ways different from today, in light of the immense transformations, in particular, within the technological order, experienced in our era. The ideal would involve modifying the planning of built spaces on the basis of the institutional and functional transformations that the future has in store.

In this respect, an ecosophical reconversion of urbanistic and architectural practices could become completely decisive. The Modernist objective has for some time been that of a standard dwelling derived from so-called "fundamental needs determined once and for all." I think here of the dogma that constituted what is called the "The Athens Charter" (1933) representing a

12. James Gleick, *La théorie du chaos* (Paris: Albin Michel, 1989).
13. Ilya Prigogine and Isabelle Stengers, *Entre le temps et l'éternité* (Paris: Fayard, 1988).

synthesis of the work of CIAM (International Congress of Modern Architecture), on which Le Corbusier published his commentary ten years later, and which was the theoretical credo for several generations of urbanists. This perspective of universalist modernism is finally in the past. Polysemic and polyphonic artists, who need to become architects and urbanists, work with a human and social matter that is not universal; but rather, with individual and collective projects evolving more and more rapidly and whose singularity, understood aesthetically, must be updated through a genuine maieutic, in particular bringing into play the procedures of institutional analysis and the exploration of unconscious subjective formations.[14]

Under these conditions, architectural design and urbanism must be considered in terms of their evolution, in their dialectic. They are called upon to become multidimensional cartographies for the production of subjectivity. Collective aspirations are changing and will change tomorrow more and more quickly. It is necessary that the quality of production of this new subjectivity becomes the primary aim of human activities and, at this point, it demands that appropriate technologies are put in its service. Such a recentering is not only a concern of specialists but also requires a mobilization of all the components of the "subjective City."

The wild nomadism of contemporary deterritorialization requires a "transversalist" apprehension of an emergent subjectivity, an apprehension that successfully articulates points of singularity (for example, a particular configuration of the terrain or of the environment, of specific existential dimensions, how children or the physically handicapped or mentally ill see space), virtual functional transformations (for example, pedagogical innovations), all affirming a style, an inspiration, that will recognize, at first glance, the individual or collective creator's signature. Architectural and urbanistic complexity will find their dialectic expressions in

14. Guattari's parenthetical remark: "It is satisfying to see how many young Japanese architects are not rushing toward the decadent way of "post-modernism," but toward what I call the way of resingularization. The coefficients of creative freedom which are the carriers of design are called upon to play an essential role in the work of the architect and urbanist. This factor manifests its dazzling role today in the firms of creators like Shin Takamatsu, Toyo Ito or groups like Team Zoo. But it does not signify, under aesthetic pretexts, an eclecticism that renounces every social vision!"

design technology and planning – from now on aided by computers – that will not close in on itself, but will articulate itself within the ensemble of the collective assemblage of enunciation that is its aim. The building and the city constitute types of objects which are carriers of subjective functions, of partial "objectities-subjectities." These functions of partial subjectivation that urban space presents to us, will not be abandoned to the risks of the property market, to technocratic agendas and the middlebrow tastes of consumers.

All these factors need to be taken into consideration, but they must remain in a mutual relation to one another. They require, across the interventions of the architect and urbanist, elaboration and interpretation – in the sense that an orchestra conductor brings to life musical phylums in a constantly innovative way. This partial subjectivation, in a sense, will have the tendency to cling to the past, to some cultural influences and reassuring redundancies, but, in another sense, it will remain attentive to elements of surprise and innovation in its way of looking, even if that is a little destabilizing. Such points of rupture, such hotbeds of singularization, cannot be taken up through simple consensual procedures and ordinary democratic processes. It means, in brief, bringing about transfers of singularity from the artist-creator of space to collective subjectivity. In such a manner, the architect and urbanist find themselves, on the one hand, wedged between the chaotic nomadism characterized by uncontrolled urbanization, or uniquely regulated by technocratic and financial dictates, and, on the other hand, between their own ecosophic nomadism that manifests itself across their diagrammatic projectuality.

This interaction between individual creativity and the multiplicity of material and social constraints, however, places a sanction on truth: there exists, in effect, a crossing of a threshold by means of which the architectural object and the urbanistic object acquire their own consistency as subjective enunciators: choose life or remain dead!

The complexity of the position of the architect and urbanist is extreme, but fascinating when their aesthetic, ethical and political responsibilities are taken into account. Immersed in the consensus of the democratic City, it is up to them to pilot by their design and their intention, the definitive bifurcations determining the fate of the subjective City. Either humanity, with the help of the architect and urbanist, will reinvent its urban future, or it will be condemned to perish under the weight of its own immobilization, that today threatens to render it helpless in facing the extraordinary challenges with which history confronts it.

Part II
Critical Essays

Pathic Transferences and Contemporary Japanese Art

by Gary Genosko

In order to understand Félix Guattari's sense of pathic transference as it appears in his final book *Chaosmosis*, I will look back at a work from the late 70s, *The Machinic Unconscious* – Guattari's work book for *A Thousand Plateaus* – and in his functional and diagrammatic deployment of the concept in the most elaborate systematic and formal expression of his analytic position in *Schizoanalytic Cartographies*; this latter work is the foundation for the more popular exposition in *Chaosmosis*. My work will be initially expository and may be contextualized in terms of how it contributes to a critical appreciation of his deployment of the pathic as a key concept extracted from phenomenological psychiatry. I am interested in developing the importance, for Guattari, of the thought of Viktor von Weizsäcker's theorization of pathic vitality. I am in this regard following a trail opened by Peter Pál Pelbart in recognizing that the pathic dimension is a mode of lived experimentation intimately connected with the self-founding and self–moving Guattarian subject living "more on the modalities of 'existensifying' than on ontic determinations."[1] Through this insight Pelbart introduces a fundamental distinction for von Weizsäcker between pathic and ontic determinations and

1. Peter Pál Palbert, "The Deterritorialized Unconscious," in *The Guattari Effect*, eds. E. Alliez and A. Goffey (London: Continuum, 2011), p. 75.

Guattari's turn inward in relation to this dichotomy. In short, I want to map some of the undertraveled pathways along this trail system of influence and deviation.

The goal of this essay is to integrate how pathic understanding applies to Guattari's interest in a number of contemporary Japanese artists including dancer Min Tanaka, painters Yayoi Kusama and Toshimitsu Imai, and architect Shin Takamatsu.

Discourse Is Not the Enemy

Guattari's schizoanalytic cartography is built around four ontological functions. One of the major divisions of these functions is drawn between a domain that is discursive, involving actualization on the plane of expression, and one that is non-discurive, that is, virtualization on the content plane. The two functions associated with the discursive order are the fluxes and machinic phylum. Both of these are sources or roots of expressions like machinic propositions of logic or computer code. Importantly, machinic propositions are not easily tied down to discursive coordinates of structuralist interpretations, including binary value-giving axes and the presupposition of differential and oppositional relations, because the machine for Guattari eludes structure; whereas existential territories and incorporeal universes belong to the non-discursive domain. Non-discursivity is by definition pathic. Pathic apprehension of being-in-the-world is not primarily discursive (neither located spatio-temporally nor describable as such) but it is *inevitably* discursive; that is, not ultimately, not forever so, but secondarily so. This is a complex relationship. Readers of *A Thousand Plateaus* will recall that the discursive is already in the body-without-organs,[2] which is basically non-discursive, that is, non-interpretive, and that discourse introduces significance, and subjectivation, both kept in "small supplies." Similarly, he positions the infinite speeds of the virtual as already loaded (pregnant or inhabited) with finite speeds[3]

---

2. Deleuze and Guattari, *A Thousand Plateaus*, trans. B. Massumi (Minneapolis: University of Minnesota Press, 1987), p. 160.

3. Guattari, *Chaosmosis*, trans. P. Bains. and J. Pefanis (Bloomington: Indiana University Press, 1995), p. 112.

of the actual (slows down, organizes, crystallizes)[4] thus, grasping finitely is possible only if an infinity upon expulsion from its domain bears a quality (reduced speed) that is graspable. Likewise, the non-discursive births the discursive, which already inhabits it, by achieving a relative consistency, and this is accomplished despite discourse's eventual penchant for delimiting non-discursivity as the snatching up becomes a holding – the consistency hardens and it mounts separations with assurances of its soundness through claims about the superiority of its method or types of evidence.

Understood as markers of discursivity, such "small supplies" include within the domains of flux (fluctuations) and phylum (the formation of fluxes) extrinsic elements of discursive ordering (exo-references) such as space-time coordinates and the linguistic formation and deformation of unformed matter,[5] that is, transformations of contingent fluxes into possible occurrences (abstract machines) and their expression as concrete machines. Guattari defines discursivity as the "synonym of sequential order exo-referenced to Energetico-Space-Time (EST) coordinates"[6] in either machinic expressions of rhizomes (knots and squares) or linear chains (levels and thresholds).

In an interview near the end of his life, Guattari explained that discourse was not the enemy. Rather, only discourse that contributes to capitalistic subjectivation – its intensive, subsumptive, expansion in immaterial labor rendered perilously precarious – is the enemy because the more it proliferates in the spread of information, the further it diminishes and slows down enunciative capacity by making it less collective, more standardized, and exchangeist.[7] Guattari invokes mythical narratives like Freudian psychoanalysis that allow fluxes to come to expression and to flow through them, only to rather "insidiously" trap them[8]; conversely, Freudian psychoanalysis promotes and supports the passages of universes of reference and gives them consistency, as in

---

4. On this point see Simon O'Sullivan, *On the Production of Subjectivity: Five Diagrams of the Finite-Infinite Relation* (London: Palgrave Macmillan, 2012), pp. 99-100.

5. Guattari, *Schizoanalytic Cartographies*, trans. A. Goffey (London: Bloomsbury, 2013), p. 131.

6. Guattari, *Schizoanalytic Cartographies*, p. 70.

7. Guattari, "The Vertigo of Immanence: Interview with John Johnston," in *The Guattari Effect* (London: Continuum, 2011), p. 36.

8. Guattari, *Schizoanalytic Cartographies*, p. 43.

the "anti-positivist" theory of jokes or in the lapsus.[9] Discourse provides support in discernibilizing non-discursive virtual enunciative content. Guattari describes the promise of this support as a "diversion of narration."[10]

Guattari was fascinated with the Japanese resingularization of architectural style, especially the work of Shin Takamatsu that opens a "third way" between a context senstive Le Corbusian modernism of house-machines embedded in highly rationalized and planned urban tissues, and detached objects of Miesian functionalism. In his writings on architectural enunciation and machinic becoming in Takamatsu's works like *ARK* dental clinic (1983), Guattari invokes "the position of a Butoh dancer like Min Tanaka, totally folded into his own body and, however, hypersensitive to all perceptions emanating from the environment."[11] Summarizing Guattari's argument, the becoming machine of *ARK* displays a nonhuman subjecthood and enunciates by means of segments of human subjectivation, both individual and collective, with which it works. Some of these segments like ocular structures, involving faciality effects, as deployed by the architect, attain a certain degree of autonomy. *ARK* achieves, for Guattari, a kind of enunciative autonomy at a certain point in the creative process of the project, and once detached from its author (architect and builder), causes contextual mutations in its neighborhood, which in turn recomposes the existential territories of its viewers, who enter into the heterogeneous enunciative assemblages of collective subjectivation. A key element of Guattari's aesthetics is a de-centering or perhaps decomposition of the human, either in the direction of an autonomization of a proto-subject, or through the loss of anthropocentric perception through an animal or vegetable becoming. Indeed, this is what Guattari is getting at in his dialogue with Tanaka, "Body-Assemblage" (included for the first time in English translation in this volume)[12] about the strategy of dancing horizontally and creeping on the ground, in the process deterritorializing his visual and auditory senses, and those of the audience as well. However, Tanaka insists upon fluctuation from the horizontal, and refuses the "horizontal" and "vertical" as standards, preferring the slanted,

9. Guattari, *Chaosmosis*, p. 26.
10. Guattari, *Chaosmosis*, p. 61.
11. Guattari, "The Architectural Machines of Shin Takamatsu," in this volume, p. 80
12. Guattari, "Body-Assemblage: Dialogue with Min Tanaka," in this volume, p. 46-47.

and leaning; consistent with this, Guattari argues that transversality rejects both a simple horizontality (field of distributions) and pure verticality (hierarchical-pyramidal) for the sake of a dynamic diagonal.[13] Tanaka's vision of becoming is insistently dynamic, and he rejects any sense it may carry of imitation (facile non-human becomings), or diminishment of change. Tanaka's hypersensitivity to the non-human components of the theatrical assemblage brings Guattari to the point of distinguishing between a representational discursive ensemble consisting of space, time, and body as well as a non-discursive non-representational domain without a substantial body – rather, a body-without-organs that is unorganized but attracts fluxes that swarm over it. Existence is produced at a pivot point between relatively unformed fluxes of sensible and semiotic matters that are instantiated within their own domain by modular screens (rhizomes) and given territorial substance (not fully formed, but proto-enunciative), and then turned back partially formed as expressive assemblages for a machinic possibilization, that is, an exploration of the potentialities of their most deterritorialized and highly charged components, their molecular elements; thus, between fluxes and phyla via territories there is a triangle of matter, form and substance. These have polysemiotic matters of expression, mediated by any site where a Tanaka dance occurs, let's say the shoreline, water, breezes, sky, humidity, etc., the so-called "winds" of matter-fluxes of dance as he performs an improvisational body-weather.[14]

Guattari's Tanaka is wrapped-up like a building in machinic becoming, yet open to the diverse "winds" that are formed by fluctuating matters in relation to which the dancer himself is decentered and into whose shifting relations viewers enter; as Tanaka puts it, the "event that happens outside of me" but with which he fuses. Moreover, Tanaka's closedness remains open like a Takamatsu building because it contains more than itself, its potential connections, what Brian Massumi refers to as the "body's vital self-abstraction" in performance understood as an unfurling diagram of its potentialities.[15] The discursive and non-discursive

13. Guattari, *Psychanalyse et transversalité* (Paris: Editions François Maspero/La Découverte, 1972/2003), p. 79.
14. Guattari, "Butoh" in this volume, p. 43.
15. Massumi, *Semblance and Event: Activist Philosophy and the Occurent Arts* (Cambridge, MA: The MIT Press, 2011), p. 140.

domains, which Guattari is describing in terms of bi-directional interfaces at infinite speeds (with qualifications) between complex actualized fluxes and hypercomplex chaosmic Territories, as well as virtual Universes and the machinic Phylum, underlines a basic principle, as stated in *Chaosmosis*:

> … what gives consistency to […] discursive systems, what authorizes the erection of enunciative monads should be sought on the side of Content; that is, on the side of this existential function which, taking support from certain discursive links, diverts them from their signifying, denotational and propositional incidences, making them play the role of a refrain of ontological affirmation.[16]

There is a diversion of discursivity from its significational entrapment in denotational and connotational semiological strata (like Barthes's staggered systems[17]) by the insurgent forces of chaosmosis that lead them, perhaps ride them, into richer and more heterogenetic enunciations that do not get stuck in the linear discursivity – a good Guattarian example of slowing down – of the syntagm, but can themselves receive grafts that highlight enriching "wild flights" and maximize "new charges of complexity."[18] Hence, Guattari's language of interface is also a negotiation.

Pathic Subjectivation

Guattari posed the following semiotic question and placed it at the heart of his conception of subjectivation: "How do certain semiotic segments achieve their autonomy, start to work for themselves and to secrete new fields of reference?"[19] This is a basic question firstly about how such segments escape being reductively beholden to structural organization and the linguistic signifier. But, secondly, it is also a question about autonomisation in an aesthetic sense. Mixing conceptual languages Guattari

---

16. Guattari, *Chaosmosis*, p. 60.
17. Barthes, *Elements of Semiology*, trans. A . Lavers and C. Smith (New York: Hill and Wang, 1967), p. 89ff.
18. Guattari, *Chaosmosis*, p. 111.
19. Guattari, *Chaosmosis*, p. 13.

settles on "partial enunciator" to express how a fragment of a work's content becomes detached from its expressive material and is seized upon by a "creative subjectivity" in the process of assembling itself – a process that involves entering a new universe that is incorporeal as it comes into existence. Such a universe doesn't pre-exist entry into it. Guattari borrows an example of this fragment of content from Bakhtin's analysis of poetry where "the feeling of movement" such as rhythmical elements become "attractors" that send processes of subjectivation down untried paths rather than back to pre-established coordinates. This "feeling of movement" is a vitality affect in the late psychotherapist Daniel Stern's terminology, a feeling unanchored to a signal of emotion (i.e., due to anger).[20] For Guattari, the detached fragment of semiotic content is a point of origin that effects a "poetic-existential catalysis" toward the emergence of "nuclei of subjectivation" and is not peculiar to either creator or audience, but rather, is "quasi-synchronically the enunciative crystallization of the creator, interpreter and the admirer of the work of art."[21] Guattari underscores the dynamic affective relations between these figures and how they are put to work creating a "new existential edifice."[22]

The figure of von Weizsäcker appears in a footnote in *The Machinic Unconscious* that warns against the tendency to fall back upon hard and fast distinctions like those between "pathic" and "ontic," or the personal-vital-fluctuations and the physical-objective world of causal relations and quantities, to which Guattari himself is sometimes prone, he readily admits. "Certain distinctions that seem relevant in a given context can function elsewhere [when they are imported from the sciences] as concepts that binarize the assemblages while aborifying the problems."[23] This is to be avoided, and one of the functions of the molar-molecular dyad, without privileging either term, is to prevent hardening from occurring that drains away all interaction. An additional point for Guattari is that the reuse of imported concepts from science cannot preserve the heterogeneity, that is, the "machinic

20. Genosko, *Aberrant Introduction*, pp. 52-3.
21. Guattari, *Chaosmosis*, p. 19.
22. Guattari, *Chaosmosis*, p. 20.
23. *The Machinic Unconscious*, trans. T. Adkins (Los Angeles: Semiotext(e), 2011), p. 149.

creationism" that he finds at every level of the cosmos.[24] Guattari regains the pathic from von Weizsächer's opposition, and finds it at work in all processes of subjectivation. Thus, by the period of *Chaosmosis*, Guattari restates his position in this way: rationalist and capitalist subjectivations can crowd out pathic knowledge by "bracketing" it as in scientific modeling.[25] He doesn't call these ontic determinations of pathic knowledge, but they perform in ways similar to impositions of objective measures on self-founding such as causes and effects.

A productively self-positing process is performed relationally in terms of points of reference like the body and the social group, and is also shaped by multiple alterities and the transit of autonomous affects and social constructions that outline constraints such as models of identity, and redundancies that define various kinds of competences. This is where the fragments of content do their work against the dampening chains of redundancies or, more interestingly, by performing the operation upon fragments of them, by extracting and then converting these to partial enunciators by "refraining" as Guattari suggests.[26] This holds them together and permits a process of subjectivation to get ahold of them for existential instantiations and incorporeal flights. The material at issue here ranges widely and Guattari gives examples from repetitive music (minimalism), Butoh dance, and Duchamp's reliance on the spectator's refinement of a work, in addition to the examples from poetics he began with. Guattari's appeal to a-signifying existential functions, indeed, to an entire "regime" of a-signification, in virtue of their relative autonomy from meaning, is less organic, and more purely informatic, than his construction of them in *The Machinic Unconscious*, where such functions grow like "microscopic parasites" on the "manure" of signification, conscientialization and modes of capitalistic subjectivation.[27] A-signifying semiotics that do not require passage through, and are not bound to meaning, encourage such mushrooming. Of course, any fragment can become enslaved cybernetically through semiotic standardization at the level of expression or suffer semiological subjection at the hands of

24. Guattari, *Machinic Unconscious*, p. 155.
25. Guattari, *Chaosmosis*, p. 26.
26. Guattari, *Chaosmosis*, p. 20.
27. Guattari, *The Machinic Unconscious*, p. 51.

various recuperative redundancies at the content level. Guattari follows Louis Hjelmslev in requiring a-signifying chains to be composed of scientifically formed matters, but not linguistically formed. Guattari's construction of an a-signifying semiotics is not a diminishment of signifying semiologies of language but rather is part of a larger scheme of "decentering." That sign machines function "directly within material and social machines without the mediation of significative processes of subjectivation"[28] is a decentering of enunciation from the human subject to machinic, non-human assemblages of enunciation. Decentering human subjectivity for the sake of machinic proto-subjectifications is one of the theoretical goals of the *The Machinic Unconscious*. For Guattari, the field of a-signification becomes that of non-human enunciation in and among machinic systems: strictly speaking, "equations and plans which enunciate the machine and make it act in a diagrammatic capacity on technical and experimental apparatuses."[29] This vast region includes the fetch-and-execute cycles of machine language, system interoperability at different levels of exchange, and multi-leveled cybernetic loops, which are scientifically formed by computer scientists and systems engineers. Enunciative machinic substances synthesizing heterogeneous qualities can also be from non-human species like birds (the Brown Stagemaker example[30]) or, as he announced in *The Machinic Unconscious*, computers can become more bound up with enunciation (think of Apple's "Siri") thereby blurring the distinction between "human creativity and machinic invention."[31] The convergence of a-signification and a-subjectification is achieved most clearly in the critique of anthropocentrism through technology but also through ethology. And with this comes an emphasis on animism (Guattari notes the animal-animist connective tissue in his conversation with Tanaka and elsewhere) through the example of self-enunciative machines at the interfaces of the discursive and non-discursive domains.[32] This, for Guattari, is the artist's contribution: extracting a fragment from the real that functions

---

28. *Ibid.,* p. 68.
29. Guattari, *Chaosmosis,* p. 36.
30. Deleuze and Guattari, *A Thousand Plateaus,* p. 331.
31. Guattari, *The Machinic Unconscious,* p. 103.
32. Angela Melitopoulos and Maurizio Lazzarato, "Machinic Animism," *Deleuze Studies* 6.2 (2012): 224.

as a partial enunciator for creator, viewer, and user: "What is important is to know if a work leads effectively to a mutant production of enunciation."[33] What Guattari found compelling in the "rich affects" of the paintings of Yayoi Kusama was their capacity to "guide us in the exploration of vegetal and vegetative virtualities that haunt our subjectivity."[34] Writing against the grain of typical psychoanalytic interpretations of her work, and even her own self-analyses of narcissism and autism, Guattari refocuses on her "decomposition of matters, forms, colors and significations up to a necessary and sufficient point from which she will then recompose vectors of sensibility and of sense of a much greater scope than those with which she initially began." While Kusama has advertised her artistic process as one of self-obliteration through the proliferation of polka dots and tiny brush strokes, at the same time she has complained of the uselessness of Freudian analysts. The play of indifferentiation and subsequent elaboration underlines the controlled character of Kusama's chaoticizations toward the production of "hypercompex affects." These affects are not describable as "undifferentiated energy" or "brute unformed matter," but instead emerge from their non-discursive domain bearing "infinite" riches of potentiality; indeed, this is Kusama's language as well as Guattari's, the former using polka dots, and latter using speeds. Kusama's paintings have the power, for Guattari, in snatching materials from an otherwise trivial consumer culture, in combination with some of the traditions of Japanese painting, to "re-enchant our world." Having lived through the "creations-destructions" of the Beat Generation and surviving the phallocratic world of abstract expressionism, Kusama's triumph as a contemporary artist is precisely in her mastery of the entities that take shape with the slowing down of the infinite speeds of a pre-objectal entity through its re-entry into the discursive atmosphere, as it were, with exquisite control over the components of a pulverized matter, which in their turn provide viewers with "new existential supports" for auto-productive subjectivations.

The most compelling implication of decentering is that it permits "enunciation [to] become correlative not only to the emergence of a logic of non-discursive intensities, but equally to

33. Guattari, *Chaosmosis*, p. 131.
34. Guattari, "The Rich Affects of Madam Yayoi Kusama," in this volume, p. 75.

a pathic incorporation-agglomeration of these vectors of partial subjectivity."[35] Guattari's shift to the non-discursive not only escapes models of subjectivity built upon discursive logics, individuation, and personhood, but pushes past the subject-object opposition. Yet drawing upon both phenomenology and psychoanalysis, Guattari looks for fusions of subject-object poles in "subjective transitivism" or "non-discursive transitivism" that do not exist outside of some relation to the discursive, but are not fixed by it or anything else for that matter. Discursivity is not the enemy done away with once and for all – it is precisely this kind of thinking that Guattari wants to avoid. Guattari instead focuses on the pathic knowledge of non-discursive experience that he mentions briefly may be seen in hypnosis and in the experience of duration in the encounter with nuclei of subjectivation that preexist the subject-object relational division. Subjectivation comes to exist alongside the subject-object relation in due course as it attempts to self-actualise. To do this it needs spatio-temporal coordinates and semiotic mediations, namely, discursive operators. But Guattari notes that this recourse to discourse has a peculiar character since although it allows for the apprehension of subjectivity's auto-formation, it additionally reveals an element of pseudo-discursivity and pseudo-mediation installed at the foundation of the subject-object relationship.[36] The paradox, as he calls it, is that the foundation of all modes of subjectivation is the pathic, even though the pathic tends to be squeezed out of discourse, especially by reductionistic sciences and rationalist subjectivities, even by badly botched narrative refrains like those of consumer culture; yet Guattari's insight is that discourse rests upon the very thing it attempts to evacuate, namely, non-discursivity. And conversely, the non-discursive requires discursivity in making lines of heterogeneity discernible.

Non-discursive universes of reference are virtual: deterritorialized and incorporeal. The virtual (complex incorporeal Universes) brings about actualization (real chaosmic existential Territorializations) by finding an interface (a complex, heterogenetic refrain, that is limitless). The operator between these two orders, that is, territory and universe, is called "pathic" – its role is to translate, back and forth, their endo-references to existential and virtual

35. Guattari, *Chaosmosis*, p. 22.
36. *Ibid.*, p. 26.

striations and in so doing mix them (i.e., mix speeds); whereas, the "ontic operator" hinges flux and phylum with exo-referenced coordinates that generate intermediary mixtures of consistencies including regularities, molding, and processual elements as well.[37] The search for nuclei of enunciative consistency involves a "diverting" deployment of discursivity (i.e., using narrative to establish complex refrains as opposed to offering explanations). Pathic knowledge does not generate objective descriptions and circumscribed fields of references with regard to external objects. For Guattari, "pathic expression is not placed in relations of discursive succession in order to situate the object in the basis of a clearly delimited referent. Here we are in a register of co-existence, of crystallization of intensity."[38] Pathic relationships are not fixed by signification, structural coordinates, or metaphysical dualisms. A virtual universe cannot be only identified in its existential incarnation; it cannot solely be described in the discursive register it deploys, fixed by its referents. The deployment of discursivity against its tendency to evacuate pathic knowledge gives to it a certain against the grain texturality as narrative, especially mythic theories like Freudianism, or those delirious narratives of psychotic patients, that can become the existential supports for intensive refrains and thus for mutant subjectivations. Nevertheless, in directing pathic intensity toward a distinctly formed and fixed entity, it may be converted into a functional anchor like a category (an abstract affect tied to a specific emotion). Guattari thinks this is the main failure of the Lacanian signifier, which inherits linearity and misapplies it in a homogenizing manner to the "pathic, non-discursive, autopoetic character of partial nuclei of enunciation,"[39] reducing the diverse components of any assemblage by means of structural logic and limiting subjectivation under the crushing weight of the symbolic order.

How does awareness of partial enunciators arise? Pathic consistencies are becomings. They are not apprehended through representation but through affect and a constantly changing field of forces that display various degrees of differentiation: "They start to exist in you, in spite of you." They transport, that is, sweep you away, Guattari thinks, into a universe of reference:

37. Guattari, *Schizoanalytic Cartographies,* p. 112.
38. Guattari, *Chaosmosis,* p. 30.
39. *Ibid.,* p. 72.

"I find myself transported into a Debussyst Universe...."[40] This happens simultaneously, before the traits of the affects enter into representational discourse. The "transversal flash" across subject and object is described by Guattari in terms of the "agglomeration" of affects before representation – it is "existence" pure and simple. Agglomeration becomes something of a technical term in *Chaosmosis* as it specifies the amassing in a jumbled, non-sequential way of components into assemblages of subjectivation. Returning to the aesthetic example of the fragment of content discussed earlier, there is a dovetailing of the transversal flash and manner in which such a fragment "'takes possession of the author' to engender a certain mode of aesthetic enunciation."[41] The transversal flash is a complex refrain that has multiple powers: "plunging" (into sadness) or "imploding" (personality).

Transitivist and Fusional

Von Weizsäcker explains his conception of the pathic in terms of five categories constituting an interdependent pentagram of verbs: may, can, will, must, shall.[42] Pathic experience finds expression through the categories modeled on verbs. The expression is fixed by verb categories which von Weizsächer describes as akin to cages in which the passions have been imprisoned. Noting, however, their abstractness, he insists that such fixity is not to the exclusion of fluidity (after all, verbs can be conjugated and qualified by auxiliaries), but that "the imprisoned bird can take flight with its cage or the cage can take flight with the bird."[43] Pathic becoming stands against ontic givenness-ordinariness. This becoming defined by cagey verbs indicates a volitional striving, that is, drive-based categories; whereas Guattari abandoned the drives for machines, and rejected the nosological categories of psychoanalysis, as well as the aforementioned affective categories for amodals. It is not hard to imagine Guattari's further objections to these statements: both the construction of a grammatical

40. Guattari, *Chaosmosis*, p. 93.
41. *Ibid.,* p. 14ff.
42. Von Weizsäcker, *Pathosophie*, trans. J. de Bisschop, M. Gennart, M. Ledoux, B. Maebe, C. Mugnier, A-M Norgeu (Grenoble: Millon Jérôme Editions), 2011, p. 54.
43. Von Weizsäcker, *Pathosophie*, p. 55.

"axiomatic" for pathic intensity and the definition of pathic striving that is based on lack, for what is not (yet): "on ne peut vouloir que ce qui n'est pas,"[44] denounced in a global refusal in *Anti-Oedipus*: "nothing can be defined as a lack."[45] For von Weizsäcker, pathic intensity appears to be stratified grammatically in which the categories are "coagulated abstractions"[46] that are only fluid as encumbered wholes (the flight of the bird in its cage). The five categories are to the logic of language what the axioms are to geometry."[47] The semiotic overcoding at work here takes language as the dominant model of realization, and the postulates can only flow as wholes and in accordance with existing rules of combination, in other words, with the imperatives of grammar as a model of subjectivation beginning in childhood. In fact, Guattari states that the pathic categories "mask one another by mutual disguise,"[48] yet he considers Von Weizsächer an inspiration for his own theorization.

Despite these differences, von Weizsäcker's thinking of the pathic is indexed to becoming. In *Cycle de la structure*, he advances a number of remarkable definitions of pathic becoming as potential: "The being in a state of crisis is nothing at the moment, but everything in potential."[49] Reading this in a Guattarian way, the emphasis is on passage and controlled proliferation. Intensive movements of the pathic erase the ontic: "The pathic state is basically a synonym for disappearance of the ontic; the crisis of transformation reveals the struggle to the death engaged in between pathic and ontic attributes."[50] This disappearance is for von Weizsäcker indicative of the non-translatibility of the pathic experience into those of the ontic, like space, time and causality.[51] Put differently, it is not possible to resolve categories of desire and obligation in ontic motivations or causes. Guattari rejects this and other typical antagonisms (pathic/ontic; eros/thanatos)

44. Von Weizsäcker, *Pathosophie*, p. 65.
45. Deleuze and Guattari, *Anti-Oedipus*, trans. R. Hurley et al (New York: Viking, 1977), p. 60.
46. Deleuze and Guattari, *A Thousand Plateaus*, p. 144.
47. Von Weizsäcker, *Pathosophie*, p. 54.
48. Guattari, *Schizoanalytic Cartographies*, p.109.
49. Von Weizsäcker, *Le Cycle de la Structure*, trans. M. Foucault and D. Rocher (Bruges: Desclée de Brouwer, 1958), p. 220.
50. *Ibid.*
51. Von Weizsäcker, *Le Cycle de la Structure*, p. 222.

and develops a domain with "ontic" attributes in his cartography. For his part, Pelbart emphasizes a link between the erasure of the ontic in von Weizsäcker and Guattari's sense of a "de-differentiated" chaosmotic immanence that exists before so-called coordinating "ontic" attributes like space and time.[52] Submersion into a chaosmotic state – described as a pathological spectrum by Guattari including psychosis, autism, mania, epilepsy, but also in terms of the painting of Imai – is experienced by a "pathic, existential absorption" into agglomerated, undifferentiated traits. Pelbart establishes that "in critical moments [crisis], life goes to 'the depths'; it resurges from the depths."[53] The depths are inhabited at specific nodes Guattari calls "umbilical," and these are where existential territories are incarnated and incorporeal universes are constituted as subjectivity begins to be established in and around these "points of intensification" as it re-emerges.[54] Every depth has its own specific texture, and every inhabitation has its own "signed and dated event."[55] Indeed, a Tanaka dance is much the same, as the dancer does not own it like a property, but it is registered at a specific site at a particular time: "I don't need 'my own dance.' Is there anything as such? I can live without it or I can remain a dancer without it. But this body is me, and dancing is what this body and mind do, so I say 'my dance.' But it is not 'my dance' as a proprietary property. One may just say 'the dance of such and such a date.'"[56] Further, Imai's works from a number of periods exemplified for Guattari the painting of chaosmosis: "Chaotic plunge into matter, osmosis between the gesture of abolition and complexity regained. From his period of gestural abstraction to his *Ka-cho-fu-getsu* turn, Imai has affirmed himself as a painter of chaosmosis."[57] The categories of von Weizsäcker may "modulate the pathic subject"; whereas a more orthodox analysts's so-called objective view would reaffirm the ontic. This is quite unlike a schizoanalyst, who lives pathically with his patients'

52. Guattari, *Chaosmosis*, p. 80.
53. Schotte quoted in Pelbart, "Deterritorialized Unconscious," p. 75.
54. Guattari, *Chaosmosis*, pp. 80 and 82.
55. Guattari, *Ibid.*, p. 81.
56. Jiae Kim and Min Tanaka, "Min Tanaka's Butoh: An Interview," *Theme* 7 (Fall 2006). http://www.thememagazine.com/stories/min-tanaka/
57. Guattari, "Imai: Painter of Chaosmosis," in this volume, p. 71.

passages into world-making and by submersion into them can "claim pathic access to the chaosmic thing."[58]

Concluding Remarks

Some of the best of the few characterizations of schizoanalysis that exist are from those Japanese artists promoted by Guattari. Guattari praised Kusama for "breaking through the wall of everydayness," just as he extolled Imai's plunge into the depths of chaosmotic intensity and return from his encounters with infinity: "Chaosmosis of the immediate, sensual, sexual, gesture that seizes the canvas. Chaosmosis of the mute expectation of "dripping," which evokes the performance of traditional Chinese painting when the watercolor vigorously reaches the delimitation of *tache*-territory."[59] Imai's artistic practice faces both directions between discursive complexity and non-discursive chaos and "clearly concatenates" their relations. This is living in depth: plunge into chaos and reemerge with the complexity already stirring there and, as its surfaces, find ways to enrich it with "mutant intensities" while paying attention to the chaos rebounding on it. And back again, to and fro. An architect like Takamatsu was able to originate pathic transferences through the singularities of his works' components, and these, once they achieved a machinic self-sufficiency, served as partial enunciators of aesthetic apprehension. The simplest pathic knowledge of a spatial proto-enunciation is that of an ambience, Guattari thought, which is without mediation and without reference to distinct, parceled information. This apprehension may result in a fantasy (outdated futurism of Takamatsu's machinism with its toy profiles (i.e., *Syntax*) or precipitate a depressive subjectivation (sensing the anguish oozing from the walls of a barracks-style primary school). Exterior discursive and immanent pathic affects interface and engage processes that can conduct the existential territories of those involved, not toward a pre-determined harmoniousness, and without mutilating promising singularities. What happens when these variations and access points to infinity are captured and beholden to interpretive schemas? Post-Lacanian

58. Guattari, *Chaosmosis*, p. 86.
59. Guattari, "Imai: Painter of Chaosmosis," in this volume, p. 71.

analyses of Kusama's work, consonant with Guattari's observations, gather her early infinity net paintings and later polka dot wall, performance, and installation pieces, in order to emphasize the shared spaces of the controlled marks and objects and how pathic chaosmotic transferences across the artist-viewer borderspace, in mutual transformation and co-emergence – "flash" – through partial subjectivations.[60]

60. See Bracha Lichtenberg-Ettinger, "Trans-Subjective Transferential Borderspace," in *A Shock to Thought*, ed. B. Massumi (London: Routledge, 2002), pp. 227-29; and Izumi Nakajima, "Yayoi Kusama between abstraction and pathology," in *Psychoanalysis and the Image: Transdisciplinary Perspectives*," ed. Griselda Pollock (Oxford: Blackwell/Wiley, 2006), p. 154.

Toward a Critical Nomadism?
Félix Guattari in Japan

by Jay Hetrick

Here is a non-Eurocentric view of the global multitude: an open network of singularities that links together on the basis of the common they share and the common they produce. It is not easy for any of us to stop measuring the world against the standard of Europe, but the concept of the multitude requires it of us. It is a challenge. Embrace it.

Michael Hardt and Antonio Negri[1]

The serial production and massive exportation of the white, conscious, male adult subject has always been correlated with the disciplining of intensive multiplicities that essentially escape from all centralization, from all signifying arborescence.

Félix Guattari[2]

In this essay, I hope to draw-out some critical and clinical consequences of Félix Guattari's fascination with Japan. According to François Dosse, he traveled there eight times in the 1980s where he mingled in psychiatric and political milieus and dialogued with intellectuals and artists of all shades.[3] I will situate this seeming *Japonisme* within Deleuze and Guattari's theoretical apparatus, focusing upon concepts like voyage and geophilosophy, in order to argue that Guattari's fascination with Japan should be

---

1. Michael Hardt and Antonio Negri, *Multitude: War and Democracy in the Age of Empire* (New York: Penguin, 2004), p. 129.
2. Félix Guattari, *The Machinic Unconscious*, trans. Taylor Adkins (New York: Semiotext(e), 2010), p. 157.
3. François Dosse, *Gilles Deleuze and Félix Guattari: Intersecting Lives*, trans. Deborah Glassman (New York: Columbia University Press, 2010), p. 481.

understood as much more than a latent Romanticism or Oriental-ism. Instead it could be understood as a "critical nomadism" that was a necessary detour for the development of his later thought. In particular, I will argue that his relatively unknown writings on Japanese artists are extremely important because they help to fur-ther elucidate his somewhat vague concept of an ethico-aesthetic paradigm by focusing upon concrete examples in the works of Min Tanaka, Keiichi Tahara, Yayoi Kusama, Shin Takamatsu, and Toshimitsu Imai. Ultimately, what allured Guattari to Japan was the fact that it seemed to highlight, within his scheme of Integrat-ed World Capitalism, a peculiar form of capitalism that hovered between the animist worlds of Shinto and the non-places of a neon hypermodernity. He argued that, as such, it was the "proto-typical model of new capitalist subjectivities," where subjectivity here points to immaterial universes of "a-signifying signs," to "a dimension of creation in its nascent state, perpetually in advance of itself, its power of emergence."[4] Guattari in Japan is therefore a kind of missing chapter in the development of his ideas con-cerning an ethico-aesthetic paradigm.

The critiques of Deleuze and Guattari's supposed Orientalism are well known. Christopher Miller, Gayatri Spivak, and Caren Kaplan have all argued, in their different ways, that Deleuze and Guattari's use of Orientalizing concepts – for example the con-cept of *nomadism* – "functions simply as a metaphorical margin for European oppositional strategies."[5] There have been several counter-critiques to this line of thinking that have a great deal of merit, especially for the already-converted.[6] And there are several established postcolonial scholars, not to mention writ-ers, who have defended and appropriated Deleuze and Guat-tari to different degrees and for different ends such as Édouard

4. Félix Guattari, *Chaosmosis: An Ethico-aesthetic Paradigm*, trans. Paul Bains and Julian Pefanis (Bloomington: Indiana University Press, 1995), p. 101-102.
5. Caren Kaplan, *Questions of Travel: Postmodern Discourses of Displacement* (Durham: Duke University Press, 1996), p. 88. See also Christopher Miller, *Nationalists and Nomads* (Chicago: University of Chicago Press, 1999), pp. 171-210 and Gayatri Spivak, "Can the Subaltern Speak?" in Cary Nelson and Lawrence Grossberg, eds., *Marxism and the Interpretation of Culture* (University of Illinois Press, 1988), pp. 271-313.
6. See Ronald Bogue, *Deleuze's Way: Essays in Transverse Ethics and Aesthetics* (Hampshire: Ashgate, 2007), pp. 113-165 and Simone Bignall and Paul Patton, eds., *Deleuze and the Postcolonial* (Edinburgh: Edinburgh University Press, 2010).

Glissant, Arjun Appadurai, Rey Chow, Réda Bensmaïa, and Elias Sanbar. But the debate has reached a level of polemical rhetoric that I don't wish to foster here. Rather, I'd like to revisit the concept of nomadism, as well as its reincarnation as "geophilosophy," in order to set the stage for an understanding of Félix Guattari's multiple forays to and with Japan. Even if we decide that Guattari is guilty of Orientalism or primitivism or *Japonisme* – which I'm not at all convinced is the case – we would also have to seriously consider the flip-side of these terms, which in fact have a highly *critical* dimension that has been left almost entirely untouched by critics. How far do we really get by simply labeling, for example, Paul Gauguin a primitivist? The main motivation for his many travels to the Caribbean and Polynesia was ultimately not to *represent* the authentic "savage" – a term with which he, in any case, personally identified toward the end of his life – but to escape the claustrophobic atmosphere of consumer capitalism and urbanization that haunted late-19th century Europe and that, he felt, prevented him from creating art, and indeed from living, in the first place. This critical logic seems to strongly underlie the statements by Negri and Guattari in the above epigraphs. And it is also where this article is heading, via the concept of critical nomadism. The whole point of nomadism is to attempt to resist the imperial, hegemonic form of what Guattari called Integrated World Capitalism by allowing minor subjectivities and languages to flourish at the peripheries. In this sense, it is completely aligned with post-colonial theory. It has nothing to do with representing, or "reterritorializing" onto, some antiquated fantasy of an exotic Other. Ultimately, and in a way that completely preempts Spivak's argument, Deleuze and Guattari are not interested in "speaking for" this Other, but in mapping the space of the encounter itself, which requires a new kind of semiotics that shatters the system of representation. As we shall see, this is especially poignant in the case of Guattari in Japan, which consists of a strange series of interviews, encounters, dialogues, and other modes of speaking and being *with*.

The significance of the concept of nomadism developed in *A Thousand Plateaus* has been established in the literature. However, in order for it to be useful for the project at hand, a clarification and differentiation needs to be made between a Deleuzian and Guattarian usage of this term. Here's the standard definition:

> The nomad distributes himself in a smooth space; he occupies, inhabits, holds that space; that is his territorial principle. It is therefore false to define the nomad by movement. Toynbee is profoundly right to suggest that the nomad is on the contrary he who does not move. Whereas the migrant leaves behind a milieu that has become amorphous or hostile, the nomad is one who does not depart, does not want to depart, who clings to the smooth space left by the receding forest, where the steppe or the desert advances, and who invents nomadism as a response to this challenge.[7]

But it seems quite clear that this is pure Deleuze, who had already spoken about nomadism at length in *Difference and Repetition*. Deleuze's nomadology should be taken neither too literally, as a necessarily Romantic reference to "real" nomads, nor simply as a suggestive metaphor. Rather, he develops a functional, and highly technical, definition of the *nomos*, which draws on the work of linguist Emmanuel Laroche and anthropologist Jean-Pierre Vernant. Before it was understood in the normative sense of custom or law, as in Democritus and Plato, the *nomos* referred to the unpartitioned and common land outside the boundaries of the *polis*, which was itself divided according to a geometric *logos*. This meaning of the *nomos* was later taken up in Zeno's *Republic*, securing for the Stoic the title of "the best exponent of anarchist philosophy in ancient Greece" by Peter Kropotkin.[8] Deleuze uses the term both in this early sense as well as in the sense of its root, *nemô*, which means to distribute. That is, his nomadology should be understood as employing these two aspects of the *nomos* simultaneously, against the Platonic law, such that "smooth space" implies an unpartitioned distribution. It is a nomadic *nomos*,

> a distribution which must be called nomadic, a nomad *nomos*, without property, enclose, or measure. Here, there is no

7. Gilles Deleuze and Félix Guattari, *A Thousand Plateaus*, trans. Brian Massumi (Minneapolis: University of Minnesota Press, 1987), p. 381.
8. Peter Kropotkin, *The Conquest of Bread and Other Writings*, ed. Marshall Shatz (Cambridge: Cambridge University Press, 1995), p. 236.

longer a division of that which is distributed but rather a division among those who distribute *themselves* in an open space - a space which is unlimited, or at least without precise limits.[9]

A nomadic distribution is one in which, for example, nomads traverse the smooth, unregulated expanse of the desert – beyond the confines of the Egyptian state – without themselves dividing it. For Deleuze, this functional definition can perhaps apply to actual nomadic people – "Egypt had its Hyksos, Asia Minor its Hittites, China its Turco-Mongols ... the Hebrews had their Habiru, the Germans, Celts, and Romans their Goths, the Arabs their Bedouins"[10] – as much as it can to other, more recent, constructions like Baudelaire's *flâneur* or Debord's psychogeographer. The *nomos* for him is simply a type of distribution and movement, which functions outside of any principle that organizes and defines the borders, both internal and external, of a territory. It is therefore anarchically indifferent to the *logos* that partitions Plato's ideal city where "twelve parts should radiate, dividing the city itself as well as the whole territory.... The men should also be distributed into twelve parts, in such a manner as to make the twelve parts as equal as possible with respect to the rest of their property."[11] But these smooth movements of nomadism are invoked primarily as a mode of *thought* unhinged from the supposed Truth of the models of recognition and representation that have been perpetuated as philosophy's *urdoxa* from Plato's *Theaetetus* to Descartes' *Meditations* to Kant's first *Critique*.

However, there is also a vague suggestion that this nomad thought is connected to a form of anarchist politics, which is already made in *Difference and Repetition* but continues in *A Thousand Plateaus*. In the former text, Deleuze states that philosophy is like painting since "it needs that revolution which took art from representation to abstraction. This is the aim of a theory of thought without image.... Crowned anarchies are substituted for the hierarchies of representation; nomadic distributions for the

9. Gilles Deleuze, *Difference and Repetition*, trans. Paul Patton (New York: Columbia University Press, 1994), p. 36. *Cf.* Deleuze and Guattari, *A Thousand Plateaus*, p. 480-481.
10. Deleuze and Guattari, *A Thousand Plateaus*, p. 495.
11. Plato, *The Laws of Plato*, trans. Thomas Pangle (Chicago: University of Chicago Press, 1988), p. 133.

sedentary distributions of representation."[12] The expression "crowned anarchy" comes from the title of Artaud's novelized biography of the Roman Emperor Heliogabalus and doesn't get us very far beyond suggesting some sort of connection between art, politics, and thought in general. But in a note to the section on "Nomadology" in *A Thousand Plateaus*, two types of political revolution are contrasted, which brings us back to the question concerning Orientalism. Deleuze and Guattari say that we can identify a "Western" type of revolution that is concerned with the transformation of the State as well as an "Eastern" one associated with its destruction. It is then insinuated that these may in fact be "successive phases of revolution" that "reflect the opposition between the socialist and anarchist currents of the nineteenth century." From this perspective, "transformation" in the former is understood to take place through the rise of labor power while "destruction" in the latter occurs through the nomadization of power itself. But this dichotomy between East and West, anarchism and socialism quickly collapses – in what appears to be an unresolved point of political difference between Deleuze and Guattari – when they write that "not only did many anarchists invoke nomadic themes originating in the East, but the bourgeoisie above all were quick to equate proletarians and nomads, comparing Paris to a city haunted by nomads."[13] This is why the invocation of Peter Kropotkin, the anti-Hegelian "anarchist" geographer of the Siberian steppe – who in fact always referred to himself as a communist – seems quite fitting. But ultimately, the precise political consequences of Deleuze's *nomos* remain a topic of groping speculation. More pressing for him are the consequences for the pre-philosophical image of thought, whose coordinates are redistributed by the operations of a nomadic philosophy that is at once critical and creative. "The conditions of a true critique and a true creation are the same: the destruction of an image of thought which presupposes itself and the genesis of the act of thinking in thought itself."[14] For Deleuze this anarchic "thought without image," as the name suggests, takes as its model the production of nomad art, another concept that is central to the politics of aesthetics we can extract from

12. Deleuze, *Difference and Repetition*, pp. 276, 278.
13. Deleuze and Guattari, *A Thousand Plateaus*, p. 558 n. 61.
14. Deleuze, *Difference and Repetition*, p. 139.

A Thousand Plateaus.[15] With the concept of nomadism, Deleuze is quite rigorously critiquing, as a well as simultaneously providing an alternative to, the habitual, *un*-critical model of representation upon which the logic of Orientalism, as well as much of post-colonial thought, depends. It should be understood as pointing to a powerful philosophical methodology that has connections with both art and politics.

The final chapter of *A Thousand Plateaus* ends with a section entitled "Nomad Art." Here it is tempting to read Deleuze and Guattari's poetic descriptions of nomadic "visions of the desert" – which rely heavily upon the works of T.E. Lawrence, Thomas de Quincey, and Wilfred Thesiger – as further evidence of their Orientalist tendencies. However, it is important to note that during the preparation of this book – that is, when Deleuze and Guattari were thinking deeply about nomadism, war machines, and the apparatus of capture – Guattari met Elias Sanbar, a Palestinian intellectual who discussed the guerrilla tactics of the struggle against Israeli occupation at a 1978 conference in Vincennes. Guattari subsequently introduced Sanbar to Deleuze and, according to François Dosse, this meeting led to an intense friendship that lasted until Deleuze's death.[16] For example, soon after their 1978 meeting, Deleuze wrote the first in a series of statements expressing his strong opposition to the Israeli occupation of Palestine as well as the politics of neo-colonialism in the Middle East more generally.[17] Deleuze also encouraged Minuit to publish Sanbar's journal *Revue d'etudes palestiniennes* in 1981. As if to preempt Spivak's criticism of Deleuze and Guattari in "Can the Subaltern Speak?" Deleuze said that the journal "enables [the Palestinians] to speak in a new way, neither aggressively nor defensively, but as 'equals' with the world," as "a people like any other people."[18] Sanbar has since become a diplomat for the Palestinian delegation and has dedicated his 2004 book *Figures du Palestinien: Identité des origines, identité de devenir* "to Deleuze, in

15. For a detailed analysis of nomad art, see my "What is Nomad Art? A Benjaminian Reading of Deleuze's Riegl" in *Deleuze Studies* 6.1 (February 2012), pp. 27-41.
16. Dosse, *Intersecting Lives*, p. 259.
17. Gilles Deleuze, "The Troublemakers," *Discourse* 20.3 (Fall 1998), pp. 23-24.
18. Gilles Deleuze, "The Indians of Palestine" in *Two Regimes of Madness*, trans. Ames Hodges and Mike Taormina (New York: Semiotext(e), 2007), pp. 194, 199.

homage to a perfect friendship." Furthermore, in an interview with Dosse, Sanbar emphatically claims that Deleuze and Guattari's texts were so essential for his own thinking that they were "always with me."[19] In Deleuze's essays on Palestine, he connects their struggle to the otherwise highly abstract concepts of nomadism and smooth space, linking it directly to the politics of neo-colonialism. He describes the Palestinians as a "people with neither land nor state" whose territory has been transformed "into a surveillance zone or a controlled desert" by the Israelis.[20] "From the start, Israel has never concealed its goal: to empty the Palestinian territory … clearly a matter of colonization, but not in the nineteenth-century European sense: the local inhabitants would not be exploited, they would be made to leave."[21] Again, rather than simply "reterritorialize" onto clichéd images of the Orient, Deleuze makes it very clear that the ethical, and indeed political, purpose of highlighting certain "nomadic visions" is to argue for the necessity of fabulation, the construction of other forms of existing and expressing beyond Orientalism and indeed beyond any kind of normative way of speaking. We have to

> get away from a "master's or colonist's discourse," an established discourse … in order to invent a minority discourse … what Bergson calls "fabulation." To catch someone in the act of fabulation is to catch the movement of the constitution of a people…. Was there ever a Palestinian people? Israel says no. Of course there was, but that's not the point. The thing is that once the Palestinians have been thrown out of their territory, then to the extent that they resist they enter the process of constituting a people. This corresponds exactly to … being caught in the act of fabulation. It's how any people is constituted. So, to the established fictions that are always rooted in a colonist's discourse, we oppose a minority discourse.[22]

---

19. Dosse, *Intersecting Lives*, p. 261.
20. Deleuze, "The Troublemakers," pp. 23-24.
21. Gilles Deleuze, "The Grandeur of Yasser Arafat," *Discourse* 20.3 (Fall 1998), p. 31.
22. Gilles Deleuze, *Negotiations*, trans. Martin Joughin (New York: Columbia University Press, 1997), p. 125.

For Deleuze, this fabulation is most fully worked out with the concepts of "minor literature" and the "people to come" but, as we shall see, Guattari argues for the need to develop an entirely new system of semiotics beyond the logic of representation, for which the question is no longer that of being able to speak or "speak for," but rather of allowing other, nearly unrecognizable, forms of expression to proliferate.

Another essential facet of nomadism as it is articulated in *A Thousand Plateaus*, which marks it primarily as a Deleuzian concept rather than one that originates with Guattari, is the fact that nomads "*do not move*. They are nomads by dint of not moving, not migrating, of holding a smooth space that they refuse to leave, that they leave only in order to conquer and die. Voyage in place: that is the name of all intensities, even if they also develop in extension."[23] That is, nomadism is fundamentally intensive rather than extensive. It is primarily about the (aesthetic, philosophical, scientific, but also potentially political) movements of thought rather than the "mere" physical movements one may traverse across an already striated earth. This is a point that radically distinguishes Deleuze and Guattari. The latter's philosophical methodology should also be described as nomadic or, as he would himself describe it, transversal, since it necessarily cuts across many fields, simultaneously remapping their various significances. Furthermore, like Deleuze, he employs this nomad thought more specifically to attempt to overturn the representational model of philosophy through his novel system of semiotics. He also connects this densely theoretical field with art and politics on a fundamental level and he does so by looking to examples from "exotic," far away places like Japan. However, Guattari also traveled to these places and even perhaps in some sense *needed* to travel to them. Contrary to the nomad that was Deleuze, there was a restless, existential nomadism in Guattari that seems more fundamental, indeed causally anterior to, his intensive movements of thought. For his entire adult life, Guattari was intimately involved with and informed by a series of radical political and psychoanalytic groups "too numerous to catalog, each phase of his life

---

23. Deleuze and Guattari, *A Thousand Plateaus*, p. 482.

having a slightly different texture."[24] In the 1980s, this existential searching reached a crescendo during what he called the "winter years," in which he experienced disillusion with various left and green parties in France, witnessed the imprisonment of his Autonomia comrades in Italy, the spread of ecological catastrophe around the globe, and the establishment of an uncritical postmodernism that threatened to appropriate and therefore nullify the radicality of the intellectual and political movements of '68 and '77. At this time, Guattari was actively looking – in a way that is not dissimilar to Gauguin's voyages toward the end of his life – for new concrete *sorties* from what was, for him, a hopeless and depressing climate. To this end, while contemplating a permanent move from France, Guattari made several extensive visits to Brazil and then Japan in order to establish connections with entirely different milieus.[25]

By contrast, Deleuze's personal aversion to traveling is articulated – even as he establishes the provenance of the conceptual link between nomadism and "not moving" – in his explanation of "V as Voyage" with Claire Parnet. He says that traveling, even, and perhaps especially, to meet other intellectuals is, in fact, the

> opposite of traveling. To go to the ends of the earth to talk ... to see people before for talking and to see people after for talking ... this is a monstrous image. It's a cheap rupture ... a trip is not enough to create a real rupture. If you want rupture, then do something other than travel. Nomads are people who don't travel.... Nothing is more immobile than a nomad. Nothing travels less than a nomad. But there are trips that are true ruptures.... In a sense, I feel no need to move. All the intensities that I have are immobile intensities.... There is a geo-philosophy, I mean, there are profound countries, my very own foreign lands that I don't find by traveling.[26]

24. Gary Genosko, "Know Your Enemy: From Integrated World Capitalism to Empire" in Félix Guattari, *The Party without Bosses* (Winnipeg: Arbeiter Ring, 2003), p. 15.
25. Genosko, "Know Your Enemy," p. 7.
26. Gilles Deleuze, "V as Voyage" in *Gilles Deleuze from A to Z*, trans. Charles J. Stivale (Cambridge: MIT, 2011), video.

Interestingly, he clarifies what he means by "immobile intensities" in "my very own foreign lands" in a letter to Kuniichi Uno – his former student and the main Japanese translator of his works – in which Deleuze explains how he and Guattari worked together:

> Guattari can jump from one activity to another. He doesn't sleep much, he travels, he never stops.... I am more like a hill: I don't move much, I can't manage two projects at once and the few movements I do have are internal.[27]

> [In] the experience of *A Thousand Plateaus* ... our conversations were full of ellipses and we were able to establish various resonances among the various disciplines that we were traversing. The best moments of the book while we were writing it were: music and the ritornello, the war-machine and nomads, and animal-becoming. In these instances, under Félix's spell, I felt I could perceive unknown territories where strange concepts dwelt.[28]

In an article written for *Le Monde* following Deleuze's death in 1995, Uno laments the fact that his teacher and friend never managed to visit Japan, despite a heart-felt invitation by Uno himself. Deleuze was of course drawn to certain Japanese filmmakers – and relied especially on Kurosawa, Mizoguchi, and Ozu in his description of "the crisis of action-image" – and admitted to Uno in another letter that "Japanese cinema has been a marvelous discovery for me."[29] Furthermore, Deleuze told Uno that he would have liked to have investigated, in relation to *The Fold*, Leibniz's fascination with the Orient,[30] which points to, Uno writes, a "certain sense of the exotic that I appreciate."[31] Ultimately, Uno suggests, it's "better to understand what happened between Deleuze and Japan in this virtual dimension" since, "hardly the great traveler," Deleuze understood "true

27. Gilles Deleuze, "Letter to Uno: How Félix and I Worked Together" in *Two Regimes of Madness*, p. 237.
28. Deleuze, "Letter to Uno," pp. 239-240.
29. Gilles Deleuze, "Letter to Uno on Language" in *Two Regimes of Madness*, p. 202.
30. Dosse, *Intersecting Lives*, p. 481.
31. Kuniichi Uno, "Japon: le rendez-vous manqué," *Le Monde* (10 November 1995).

nomadism as traveling in place, moving constantly but in small movements, in imperceptible flashes" that are often "more vital than grandiose historical actions."[32] Interestingly, in the same epitaph for Deleuze, Uno argues that "Guattari was much more fascinated by Japan and its singular creation of a post-industrial subjectivity, through the combination of the ultra-modern and the archaic."[33] Uno invited Guattari to Japan in 1983 and it was with his help that "Guattari was able to meet the politicized, very militant milieus in Okinawa and visit several psychiatric hospitals."[34] Ultimately, we could argue that Guattari's nomadism required real voyages, real encounters and dialogues *with* and not only about Japanese artists in order to help formulate his last ideas on aesthetics. Because the theme of Japan and Japanese art became a veritable refrain for Guattari during the 1980s, it may be useful to reframe our reading of his last work, *Chaosmosis: An Ethico-aesthetic Paradigm* (1992) – which should be understood as an example of Guattari's nomadic, or transversal, thought since it imbricates the fields of aesthetics, ethics, ontology, and politics on the same plane – through the lens of these encounters. Indeed, the "animist" ontology that grounds this ethico-aesthetics seems to come in part from his various encounters with Japan.[35] Furthermore, Toshimitsu Imai, for example, is described as the "painter of chaosmosis" par excellence.[36] During the winter years, except for brief analyses of the works of Gérard Fromanger and Balthus, Japanese figures serve as the primary examples of visual artists whose works might help us to make sense of his last, somewhat enigmatic, statement on aesthetics. In *Chaosmosis*, Guattari argues that "archaic societies are better equipped than white, male, capitalistic subjectivities to produce a cartography of multivalence of alterity," which for him was the necessary first step toward resisting new forms of capitalist exploitation and alienation.[37] He also defines his ontology of machinic assemblages in this book as

32. Uno, "Japon: le rendez-vous manqué."

33. Uno, "Japon: le rendez-vous manqué."

34. Dosse, *Intersecting Lives*, p. 482.

35. For a detailed analysis of Guattari's concept of animism, see my article "Video Assemblages: 'Machinic Animism' and 'Asignifying Semiotics' in the Work of Melitopoulos and Lazzarato" in *Footprint* 14 (Spring 2014), pp. 53-68.

36. Félix Guattari, "Toshimitsu Imai: Painter of Chaosmosis" in this volume, p. 69.

37. Guattari, *Chaosmosis*, p. 45.

depending upon an "animist revival."[38] But while he does briefly refer to Japanese Butoh dance in *Chaosmosis,* we have to look elsewhere in order to really grasp what he's trying to do here, beyond the easy charges of Orientalism or primitivism. For example, he rhetorically asks in an essay called "Tokyo, the Proud": "might Japanese capitalism be a mutation resulting from the monstrous crossing of animist powers inherited from feudalism during the 'Baku-han' and the machinic powers of modernity to which it appears everything here must revert?"[39]

In an interview with Tetsuo Kogawa in 1981, Guattari remarks that psychoanalysis merely repeats the colonialist attitude of projecting "a certain kind of interpretation of reality" onto the "new continent of subjectivity." His critique of this attitude consists in the fact that there is "something which escapes the realities of our developed societies, something which does not want to be an international movement, a school, a technique that we learn in manuals, something that forces us to reflect upon real analytic forms in the manner in which they appear."[40] This *something* is the ephemeral "object" of Guattari's most original contribution to the history of thought. Throughout his career, he sought to develop a new system of semiotics that takes into account a much broader range of possible expressions than those delineated by the Saussurean system, which not only separates the human from the non-human but also encourages the hierarchization of different sorts of human expression itself.

His interest in animism was motivated precisely by the fact that, through it, such hierarchization seems to break down. As Maurizio Lazzarato notes, "trans-individual polysemic animist subjectivity uncovers the possibility of producing and enriching ... semiotic symbols of the body, dance, postures, and gestures ... as well as a-signifying semiotics such as rhythms, music, and so on."[41] Saussurean semiotics is not abstract enough, but here abstract doesn't mean less reified because, in fact, it is only with the representational semiotics of everyday linguistics that signs become relatively cut off from their direct imbrication with

---

38. Guattari, *Chaosmosis*, p. 77.
39. Félix Guattari, "Tokyo, the Proud" in this volume, p. 12.
40. Félix Guattari, "Translocal: Tetsuo Kogawa interviews Félix Guattari" in this volume, p. 31.
41. Angela Melitopoulos and Maurizio Lazzarato, "Machinic Animism," p. 246.

matter. In Guattari's semiotics, there is a primacy of "machinic enunciation" over language and words, which only appear as the thinnest surface layer of a vast and complex assemblage that incorporates many different types of signs. There are four main semiotic registers in this system: natural a-semiotic encodings like DNA or crystalline structures; symbolic (or pre-signifying) semiologies that include bodily gestures and the rituals of archaic societies; the representational, signifying semiology of Saussure; and a-signifying (or post-signifying) semiologies, which include mathematical formulas, stock quotes, and computer languages, but also the rhythms, durations, and intensities of music, art, and film. Especially for the Guattari of *Chaosmosis*, the register of a-signifying enunciation becomes *the* field upon and through which a critical contemporary battle is waged: art against empire. In the era of what Lazzarato has called immaterial labor, art becomes important since it potentially expresses the *something* that always eludes the axiomatization of capital. The elements of a-signifying semiotics, which can be found most clearly in artistic and shamanic practices, are therefore "power signs," material particles that do not pass through linguistic chains, but rather plug into the body directly through pre-conscious affects and percepts.[42] Furthermore, they don't produce signification, they don't *speak*, but function machinically through "a direct, unmediated impact on the real," that triggers "an action, a reaction, a behavior, an attitude, a posture."[43] Ethico-aesthetics. Art potentially connects us to the realm of a-signifying semiotics – which circulates "in much the same way as 'mana' circulates in animist societies,"[44] through a logic that Guattari variously calls "contagion," "pathic transference," or "unnatural participation" – and therefore may help us escape the clutches of contemporary control society in order to develop new "practices of freedom and processes of

42. Félix Guattari, *Molecular Revolution: Psychiatry and Politics*, trans. Rosemary Sheed (London: Penguin, 1984), p. 127.
43. Maurizio Lazzarato, "Semiotic Pluralism and the New Government of Signs: Homage to Félix Guattari," trans. Mary O'Neill, online at http://eipcp.net/transversal/0107/lazzarato/en
44. Maurizio Lazzarato, "Existing Language, Semiotic Systems, and the Production of Subjectivity in Félix Guattari" in *Cognitive Architecture: From Biopolitics to Noopolitics*, ed. by Deborah Hauptmann and Warren Neidich (Rotterdam: 010 Publishers, 2010), p. 515.

individual and collective subjectivation."[45] Furthermore, the aesthetics of a-signifying semiotics plays both "a central and decisive role in contemporary capitalism and creates the conditions for its *political* critique."[46]

> These behaviors appear and disappear in public space following logics that escape the rules of 'representation'.... Their objectives are not representations or the seizure of power, but rather the transversal and molecular constitution of new sensibilities and new social relations.[47]

This is ultimately what is at stake in Guattari's fascination with Japan: a critical nomadism, where nomadism refers to a transversal mode of ethico-aesthetic thought beyond the conditions of Western high capitalism, a thought which can be qualified as critical insofar as it attempts to think beneath recognizable speech within an anarchic, or nomadic, plane of a-signifying semiotics. According to Guattari's Japanese interlocutors, and contrary to his own hopes, "the combination of the ultra-modern and the archaic ... doesn't really work anymore"[48] and, ultimately, "Japan did not become the 'capital of the emancipation of the Third World.'"[49] Nevertheless, there is indeed something potentially revolutionary about finding subaltern, animist sign-particles germinating within works of art that escape the overcoding of Integrated World Capitalism.

I'd like to conclude by changing track a bit and by suggesting that, at least in terms of finding works of art that might help further elucidate his ideas on aesthetics, Guattari had to seek out ethico-aesthetic "power signs" somewhere *other* than the Western art of the 1980s. This is perhaps due to reasons internal to the history of contemporary art, which Guattari detested, rather than any kind of latent Orientalism or exoticism on his part. Despite the fact that, for example, neo-expressionists like Georg Baselitz,

---

45. Maurizio Lazzarato, "Semiotic Pluralism."
46. Lazzarato, "Existing Language," p. 512.
47. Maurizio Lazzarato, "What Possibilities Presently Exist in the Public Sphere?" trans. Nate Holdren, online at http://www.generation-online.org/p/fplazzarato4.htm.
48. Uno, "Japon: le rendez-vous manqué."
49. Toshiya Ueno, "Guattari and Japan," *Deleuze Studies* 6 (May 2012), p. 190.

Gerhard Richter, and Anselm Kiefer were creating works in the 80s – some of which, I would argue, express the plane of a-signifying semiotics quite forcefully – they have been sometimes described as politically and aesthetically reactionary with regard to the happy postmodernism of Jeff Koons, *et al.*, that is, as anachronistic with respect to the official narrative of art history and therefore less convincing as examples of art that convey contemporary sensibilities.[50] But, more than this, Guattari believed that contemporary Western art in general is completely caught within a suffocating institutional structure that preempts any kind of circulation of affects and percepts, whether we consider neo-expressionism or postmodernism. He simply had to find something else.

> Let's just say that contemporary art remains trapped within an institutional framework. There's a universe of reference, a universe of valorization, including economic valorization, that frames the work and qualifies it as such, attaching it to a social field.[51]

Japan in the 1980s, on the other hand, had just gone through its own modernist development and the particular artists Guattari gravitated toward – Min Tanaka, Keiichi Tahara, Yayoi Kusama, Toshimitsu Imai – would most correctly be labeled as "avant-garde," a designation that was and is no longer possible in the West. So, perhaps Guattari needed these figures in order to put his, arguably modernist, aesthetics to work toward a future ethical and political paradigm under the conditions of an Integrated *World* Capitalism.[52] It is clear that subjective, but also political, emancipation was the critical goal of everything he did, said, or wrote. And while this doesn't imply a strong teleology, Guattari's imbrication of the aesthetic, ethical, and political does seem to have a particular directionality, which begins with the

---

50. Guattari explicitly dismisses neo-expressionism and its variants in his *Schizoanalytic Cartographies*, trans. Andrew Goffey (London: Bloomsbury, 2012), p. 37.
51. Félix Guattari, "On Contemporary Art: Interview with Oliver Zahm" in *The Guattari Effect*, ed. Éric Alliez and Andrew Goffey (London: Continuum, 2011), p. 46. Translation modified.
52. See Stephen Zepke, "Art as Abstract Machine: Guattari's Modernist Aesthetics," *Deleuze Studies* 6 (May 2012), pp. 224-239.

"aesthetic perception"[53] of unformed, a-signifying matter-signs and moves through a "processual creativity"[54] that then informs "the site of a work, a potential praxis,"[55] which is finally qualified as "ethicopolitical."[56] This is why he says that the "aesthetic power of thought, although equal in principle with the other powers" of thinking, occupies "a privileged position" in our era of immaterial labor and semiocapitalism.[57]

If Japan hasn't become the capital of Third World emancipation, perhaps some of its artists do express a "geo-aesthetic" paradigm for the radical reconfiguration of subjectivity that ultimately opens onto a "non-Eurocentric view of the global multitude."[58] In their last collaborative work, Deleuze and Guattari argue that, even if we understand philosophy as a fundamentally Greek phenomenon, its pre-philosophical ground was established in an encounter "along the borders of the Orient."[59] Most directly, they are referring here to Heraclitus and the pre-Socratics who inhabited the Ionian coast but, curiously enough, they also devote the next few pages to outlining the relation between "Chinese hexagrams, Hindu mandalas, Jewish sephirots, Islamic imaginals" – that is, various Oriental diagrammatic figures – and the birth of philosophical thinking.[60] With this undoubtedly enigmatic outline for a geophilosophy – along with Guattari's ethico-aesthetic paradigm – in mind, can we understand Min Tanaka's bodily movements "in other directions of sense ... beneath industrial identities, beyond narrative programs"[61]; Keiichi Tahara's photographic "machines that undo the common sense of forms ... diagrams [that] throw us ... into a universe without foreseeable ends, without the delimitations of identity;"[62] Yayoi Kusama's

53. Guattari, *Chaosmosis,* p. 131.
54. Guattari, *Chaosmosis*, p. 13.
55. Félix Guattari, "Ritornellos and Existential Affects," in *The Guattari Reader*, ed. Gary Genosko (London: Blackwell, 1996), p. 166.
56. Félix Guattari, "Regimes, Pathways, Subjects," in *The Guattari Reader*, p. 104
57. Guattari, *Chaosmosis,* p. 101.
58. Hardt and Negri, *Multitude,* p. 157.
59. Gilles Deleuze and Félix Guattari, *What is Philosophy?* trans. Hugh Tomlinson and Graham Burchell (New York: Columbia University Press, 1994), p. 87.
60. Deleuze and Guattari, *What is Philosophy?*, p. 89.
61. Félix Guattari, "Butoh" in this volume, p.41.
62. Félix Guattari, "The 'always never seen' of Keiichi Tahara" in this volume, p. 66.

"extraordinary *dispositifs* of aesthetics and subjectivation"[63]; or Toshimitsu Imai's *informel* paintings in which "representation implodes, is diverted toward worlds where there is never a question of distinct oppositions, [toward] the immobile vibration of an a-typical, a-topical, a-chronic enunciation, hanging on the tip of an eyelash, on the wing of a butterfly, thrown into the wild java of a summer dust cloud"[64] as singular attempts to re-*fabulate* subjectivity in ways that ultimately inspire "the transversal and molecular constitution of new sensibilities and new social relations?"[65] This is the task of Machinic Eros.

63. Félix Guattari, "The Rich Affects of Madam Yayoi Kusama" in this volume, p. 74.
64. Félix Guattari, "Imai: Painter of Chaosmosis" in this volume, p. 71.
65. Lazzarato, "What Possibilities Presently Exist in the Public Sphere?"

Note on Contributors

Félix Guattari (1930-92) was a French psychoanalyst, activist-intellectual, and philosopher known widely for his collaborations with Gilles Deleuze and Antonio Negri. His books have been translated into multiple languages, including English and Japanese. His papers and personal library are held in the Institut Mémoires de l'édition contemporaine in Caen, France.

Gary Genosko is Professor of Communication at the University of Ontario Institute of Technology in Toronto. He has published extensively on Félix Guattari, Gilles Deleuze, Jean Baudrillard, and Marshall McLuhan. His most recent books are *Remodelling Communication: From WWII to the WWW*, and *When Technocultures Collide: Innovation from Below and the Struggle for Autonomy*.

Jay Hetrick is Assistant Professor of Cultural Studies at the American University in Dubai. He has published in the fields of 20th century art, continental aesthetics, and critical theory. He is currently reediting his PhD thesis - entitled *Cine-aesthetics: A Critique of Judgment after Deleuze and Michaux* - for publication and is translating Maurizio Lazzarato's *Videophilosophy* into English.

Univocal Publishing
123 North 3rd Street, #202
Minneapolis, MN 55401
www.univocalpublishing.com

ISBN 9781937561208

All materials were printed and bound
in January 2015 at Univocal's atelier
in Minneapolis, USA.

This work was composed in Garamond
The paper is Hammermill 98.
The letterpress cover was printed
on Crane's Lettra Pearl.
Both are archival quality and acid-free.